Bloom County Books by Berke Breathed

BLOOM COUNTY BABYLON:
Five Years of Basic Naughtiness

BERKE BREATHED

Bloom County BABYLON

FIVE YEARS OF BASIC NAUGHTINESS

JOHN BROWN PUBLISHING LTD.

FIRST UK EDITION 1988

FIRST PUBLISHED IN THE UNITED STATES AND CANADA
BY LITTLE, BROWN & COMPANY

BLOOM COUNTY is syndicated by The Washington Post Writers Group.

ISBN 1 870870 042

JOHN BROWN PUBLISHING LTD.

PRINTED IN SPAIN

To Sophie,
my love, my life, my dog

"I have often had the impression that, to penguins, man is just another penguin—different, less predictable, occasionally violent, but tolerable company when he sits still and minds his own business."

—*Bernard Stonehouse*

"JOIN ME IN THE HILLS!" he yelled in passing. "ONLY THE PROPERLY EQUIPPED WILL SURVIVE!"
His fatigues were freshly pressed.

The Great LaRouche Toad-Frog Massacree

by Michael J. Binkley

Adapted from *Daze of My Youth: A Bloom County Memoir,*
published by Little, Brown and Co.

THE SUMMER OF 1988 DESCENDED on Bloom County much as it had for each of the previous nine years of my life; humid and without hint of the chaos ahead. We needed no hints, however, for calamity always rode shotgun with Bloom County summers. Each spring, bored boys awaited the hot months with the giddy anticipation normally reserved for the imminent approach of a gang of Nazi motorcyclists. Things were going to *happen.* Wonderful things. Catastrophic things. And if that meant, say, that my dad's new Chrysler LeBaron were to be dynamited by Japanese antiprotectionist guerrillas, so be it. This was summer, after all, and such things simply happen. Confident in the knowledge that soon the June sun would fry most of the common sense out of everyone's noodle, Milo and I would kick back among the meadow dandelions and wait for things to generally fall apart. As I said, this summer was to be no different.

These were contented times for me, being, at age ten, still safely ignorant of what my adulthood would bring (namely, a clerkship at the lingerie counter of Wal-mart, a job that would send some fetishists I know into palm-sweating ecstasy but which, alas, still sends me to my knees with nausea. See chapter 11, "Women and Nausea"). These were, in fact, generally contented times for everyone. A presidential election was approaching, but it would be another four years before Clint Eastwood reached the White House and really stirred things up, so for the moment, life was pretty tranquil. This, I figure, helps explain the exaggerated behavior of Bloom Countians over what happened that summer.

The Great LaRouche Toad-Frog Massacree, as it became known, had its roots in two entirely separate and unrelated events: a conspiracy of happenstance which was to test the civil defense preparedness of an entire American community and forever alter the ecological food chain of the North Meadow Pond.

On June 21, 1988, the following item appeared on page 3 of the daily *Bloom Beacon,* sandwiched between an article on the plummeting price of cow tongue and "Dear Abby":

COMMUNISTS AT U.S. DOORSTEP

by Milo Bloom, Investigative Reporter

Today it was discovered that after years of aggressive expansion, the Soviet Union has stretched its borders to within a mere 12 miles of American soil. The State Department has no immediate comment.

... which wasn't particularly surprising since the State Department had been aware for some time that the easternmost tip of Siberia comes within a polar bear's whisker of Alaska, but who cares since it's too damned cold to worry about. But the vast bulk of the *Beacon's* readership had no such knowledge and a subdued rumble of patriotic consternation coursed through the local population like some frightening new flu virus. The consensus was that something ought to be done. "SOMETHING," bellowed Steve Dallas at a hastily called town meeting, "SHOULD BE DONE!" He pounded the table, looking properly drunk with nationalistic fervor. Eunice Annanburg suggested CIA assassinations of most of the Kremlin, but she was soundly overruled in favor of a more moderate response. A letter would be dispatched to the President informing him of the crisis. (Years later, Caspar Weinberger would write in his memoirs that he had been sent to the White House to reassure Mr. Reagan that it wasn't necessary to send the Sixth

Fleet to investigate this new business. We were pleased our letter had attracted the attention it deserved. The President was a fave-rave in Bloom County.)

A high level of media-inspired hysteria and paranoia having now been generated, the stage was set for the second minor incident to complete the general breakdown of order that led to The Great LaRouche Toad-Frog Massacree. And it happened early the next Sunday morning, deep within the Bloom County Volunteer Fire Department's wiring system. Several errant electrons jumped when they shouldn't have at a place they shouldn't have, resulting in what shouldn't have happened. In short, a short. The air-raid siren came to life for the first time in Bloom County history.

It must have started about 6:00 in the morning and, it being Sunday, caught everyone asleep. At least everyone in Milo's boardinghouse, where my father and I lived. Bolting upright in bed, eyes wide, I listened to the wail outside and knew immediately that this day was to be dealt a perfectly proper dose of pandemonium. The Nazi motorcyclists had, so to speak, arrived. A nuclear missile attack was not safe but it was certainly *not* boring.

"Get under the door frames!" yelled Dad, huddling beneath his as I emerged from my room. I told Dad that standing under door frames was usually something done during an earthquake and that he might have been mixing up his catastrophes—but by then the rest of the residents had emerged and were milling around the top of the staircase, listening to the siren and peering up at the ceiling. These, I later thought, are the many foolish things people do while waiting for Russian missiles.

Standing there in our various forms of undress, nobody had to say what we were all thinking. That newly discovered twelve-mile gap between our peace-loving people and the Soviet hordes had been just too tempting and the Bolsheviks had decided to get the jump on us. "I *TOLD* you all that something should have been done!" said Steve Dallas, who was pounding the wall wearing only Fruit of the Loom briefs. That Steve also was barefoot was actually the greatest danger we faced at the moment, his feet being considered a public health hazard within a five-county area. In Bloom County, prolonged bachelorhood is often looked at with suspicion, but in Steve's case it was merely a consequence of poor foot hygiene: women were simply never seen in his company. Now, Steve didn't look much like what a homosexual was generally presumed to look like, so folks accepted the foot theory and gave him little trouble as long as he kept his loafers on. Normally, aging bachelors can be a real moral strain on a small town.

The siren still screamed and Milo quickly took control of the situation. "Okay!" he said, "Where's our Civil Defense Coordinator?" This was a good question, since Opus, who held that office, was missing. . . . A quick search found him sitting on the pot with the Sunday funnies. A late night of questionable activities had apparently taken their toll, for he was asleep with the comics draped over him like a quilt. Our Civil Defense Coordinator was awakened rudely and dragged, struggling in a half nelson, to the top of the stairs.

I should digress to explain that the more unsavory positions of official authority within the boardinghouse bureaucracy were given to those members who made the unfortunate mistake of being absent for house meetings. Thus Opus, much to his eventual horror, had been given the honor of being voted Official Trash Coordinator, Official Wasp Nest Remover, Official Rain Gutter Cleaner, Official Chimneysweep, and Official Handler of Steve Dallas's Socks—positions he earned by being off somewhere in Milo's Meadow picking his nose when the nominations were made. These were underhanded actions and complaints were lodged. But this—this Official Civil Defense Coordinator business was something altogether different. That awful Sunday morning in June was the first Opus had heard about this new office. "ME?" he cried. "ME? Nope! No way. No no no! Uh-uh! ME?" He started to hyperventilate, so we wiped his brow with a cool rag and got him some herring entrails and grape juice, which calmed him down some.

With the collapse of the only official leadership, the situation began to deteriorate. Thermonuclear bombs were due at any moment, things had to be done. Panic had to be averted. Steve realized what he needed to do and returned to his room while the rest of us regrouped outside in the street. Opus, dazed and faint with anxiety, was propped up and federal civil defense instructions were shoved into his hands. Dad, Milo, his grandfather, Oliver Wendell Jones and his parents from next door, passersby in the street, all came to attention and awaited instructions. The sirens wailed on. Obviously only minutes remained.

" 'First,' " said Opus, reading from the government manual, " 'Gather shovels.' " We dispersed and looked for shovels, returning with several. " 'Second, quickly and without panic, take refuge in countryside.' " Shovels in hand, we formed an orderly line and proceeded to march behind our hyperventilating leader down the street, passing by others who were clearly reacting to the threat of thermonuclear annihilation with less self-control than ourselves. We, after all, had taken the precaution of procuring not only an official federal civil defense handbook, but an official—if reluctant—Civil Defense Coordinator as well.

Upon reaching the dandelions of Milo's Meadow, well removed, we supposed, from Ground Zero, we stood at attention and awaited further instructions. *"'Dig shallow trenches,'"* Opus continued. *"'Lie down in trenches, cover self with wooden door or like object and await blast. After shock wave passes, emerge and go to nearest emergency Civil Defense Center and fill out emergency change of address forms.'"*

With this, we seized the handbook and hacked it to pieces with our shovels. Opus was officially decommissioned and we quickly adopted a favorite stand-by approach to an approaching holocaust—hysterical panic. This is always fun to watch, so Milo and I settled back into the grass to savor the confusion, our own fates apparently sealed. Opus wrung his hands and worried about what radiation would do to his complexion.

Steve Dallas jogged by, dressed in designer fatigues and wearing an extraordinarily full backpack. "JOIN ME IN THE HILLS!" he yelled in passing. "ONLY THE PROPERLY EQUIPPED WILL SURVIVE!" Or the lawyers, we thought. "JOIN ME AND WE'LL CRAWL FROM THE RUBBLE AND LIVE TO FIGHT ANOTHER DAY. TO THE HILLS! ONLY THE WEAK WILL PERISH!" This was no comfort to a nearly shattered Opus, who had no illusions as to where he stood in the strong/weak classification. Watching his best friend Steve Dallas disappear into the woods dressed like Rambo proved the final decisive blow to an already critical frame of mind and he plopped over unconscious. Lying serenely among the clover, Opus was blessedly unaware of Portnoy and Hodge-Podge marching up the hill with a fully automatic 45mm American Ruger Assault rifle, apparently intent upon massacring the imminent hordes of Communists in groups of fifty or more. "We're gonna massacree 'em!" bellowed Portnoy, waving the weapon that had obviously been recently borrowed from the shelves of the K-Mart Sporting Goods Section. Milo and I, concluding that the general scheme of things just couldn't handle *this* much fun, tried to dissuade Portnoy and his fellow conspirator from their patriotic mission. They would not hear of it. These, after all, were a groundhog and a rabbit, two of the most excitable critters to be found in modern meadows and wont to excessive behavior. "We'll go out blasting!" they said.

Down we went, following these two warriors, to the North Meadow Pond, where invading Russians were suspected. Opus awoke and trailed this dangerous procession, rubbing his stomach, for nuclear war had upset it. If he was to die in a fireball, he thought, it would be nice to go to Heaven without gas. This was obviously not to be and the crushing reality pushed him further into a deep funk. He was nearly to the point of tears when Portnoy, aiming into the water of the North Meadow Pond where the Communists were hiding in their scuba equipment, pulled the trigger of his massacre machine. "I CAN SEE THEIR EYES! YAAAAAAA!" he screamed, or something like that. For a full minute, automatic weapon fire tore into the little pond, turning it into a horrible, savage, boiling froth of hot lead and foam. We hit the ground as the spray of bullets continued, tearing up trees, rocks, sod, an old inner tube—oh, it was simply horrific. Order was restored when the ammo was exhausted and we picked ourselves off the ground. Opus had, at the first blast, collapsed in cardiac arrest and was briefly thought to be shot, but after thorough and prolonged CPR, was brought back to full consciousness, walking away from the incident with only minor emotional troubles.

Back at the battle scene, we survivors checked for bullet holes in our clothing. Portnoy sat on his rump, the gun on his lap smoking. He surveyed the sight in front of him and quietly exhaled a low, sliding whistle, much as one might do when passing a terrible car wreck.

There, floating facedown in the turbid water, were hundreds, no, *thousands* of corpses...legs wide apart, arms spread, tongues extended their full eight or ten inches. It was plain as pie that there wasn't a single living toad-frog remaining in that pond. The overwhelming magnitude of the crime grew on us as we stood around, eyes bulging and mouths agape. "Look at Portnoy," I whispered to Milo, for indeed, the crushing realization of guilt at what he'd done came across his face like a shadow, and he slumped in shame. These tragic victims were clearly not Russians, although he could have sworn they *were* when he first saw their gleaming eyes in the early morning light.

Milo, realizing that Portnoy's emotional stability was at stake, went to his side and explained that while, admittedly, the likelihood of those toad-frogs being Communists, or even liberals, was not great, there was no reason to assume that he had wiped out supply-side Republicans instead. In fact, there was an excellent chance that the vast majority of them were LaRouche Democrats, who, of course, were better off dead.

This revelation appeared to cheer Portnoy, and the entire party headed back into town where we stopped off for Egg McMuffins, the air-raid siren having long since been silenced and the general domestic tranquillity restored. The newspapers recorded Portnoy's excesses that pandemonious day as The Great LaRouche Toad-Frog Massacree, an honor which won him some brief celebrity and a quick appearance, via satellite, on "Nightline." Things settled down soon afterward and, except for the frequency of fried LaRouche frogs' legs served at supper, normalcy returned to haunt the remaining summer.

I neglected to mention, however, that Steve Dallas was eventually discovered by a small and unenthusiastic search team several days after the Massacree, lying spread-eagled and dazed among the summer hyacinths and surrounded by the remnants of his survivalist base camp, now in a state of higgledy-piggledly. A blow-dryer, blender, toaster, piña colada mix, microwave oven, and other essentials of survival lay scattered among the barbed wire and camouflage netting. His formerly impressive fatigues were nowhere to be seen. The shocking truth is that all he was wearing was an argyle sock and a bad sunburn. Opus bent down and put an ear to Steve's mouth just in time to hear him whisper, "The horror...the horror...I...forgot...the...mayonnaise." We took him home and rubbed Noxzema all over him and put him to bed, where he remained for the better part of the week stuck to the sheets.

15

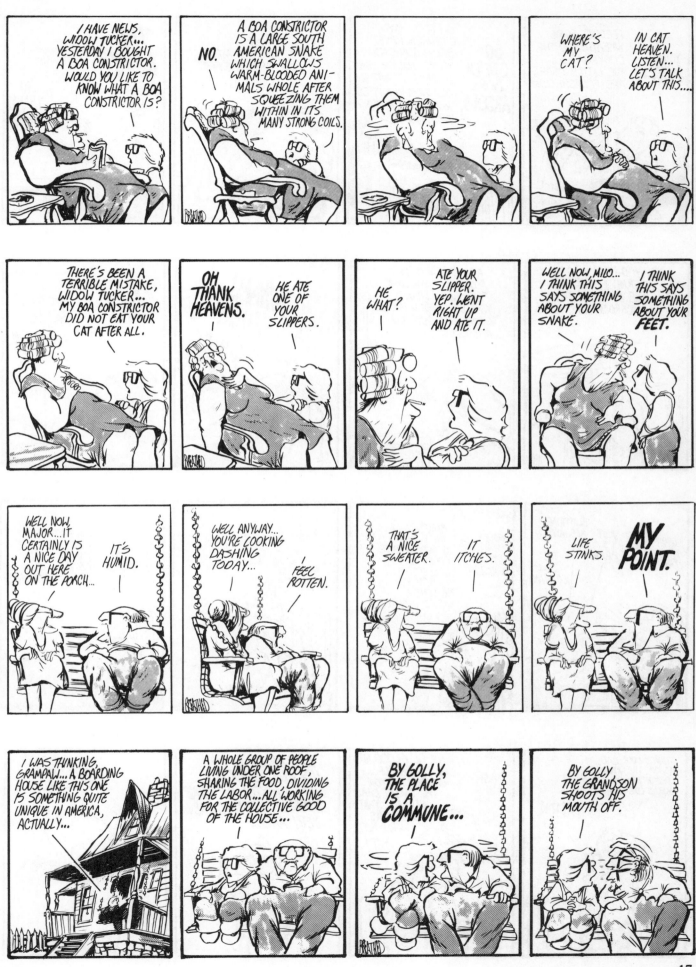

17

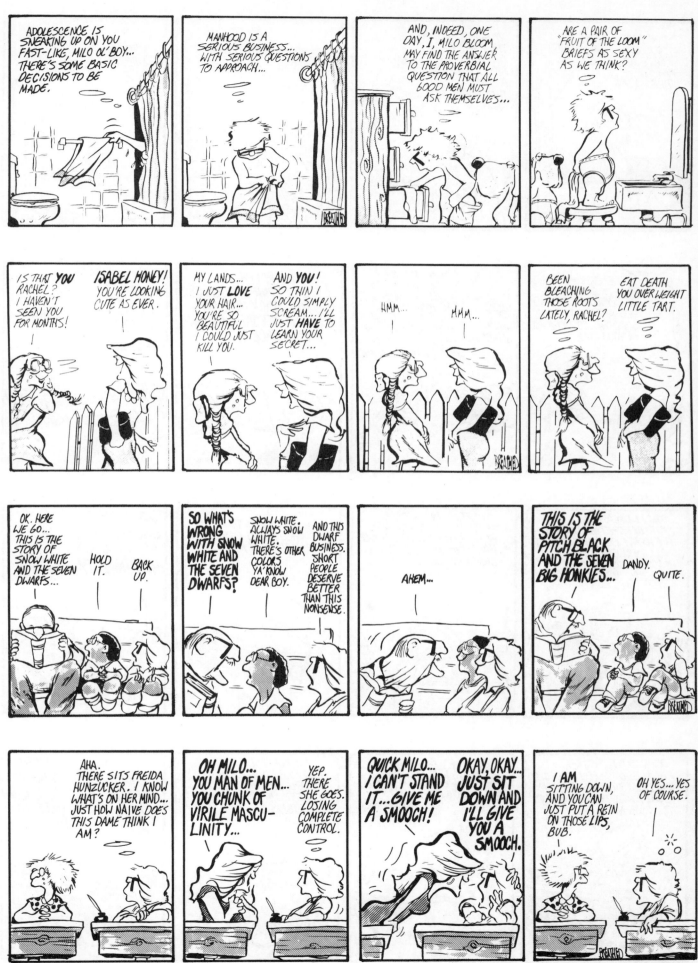

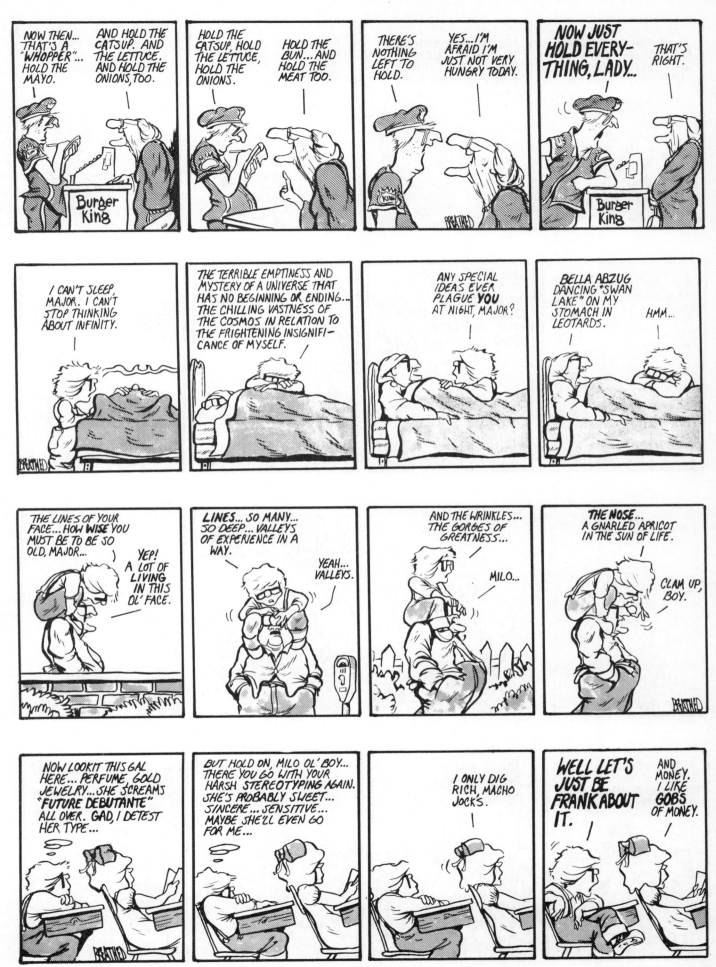

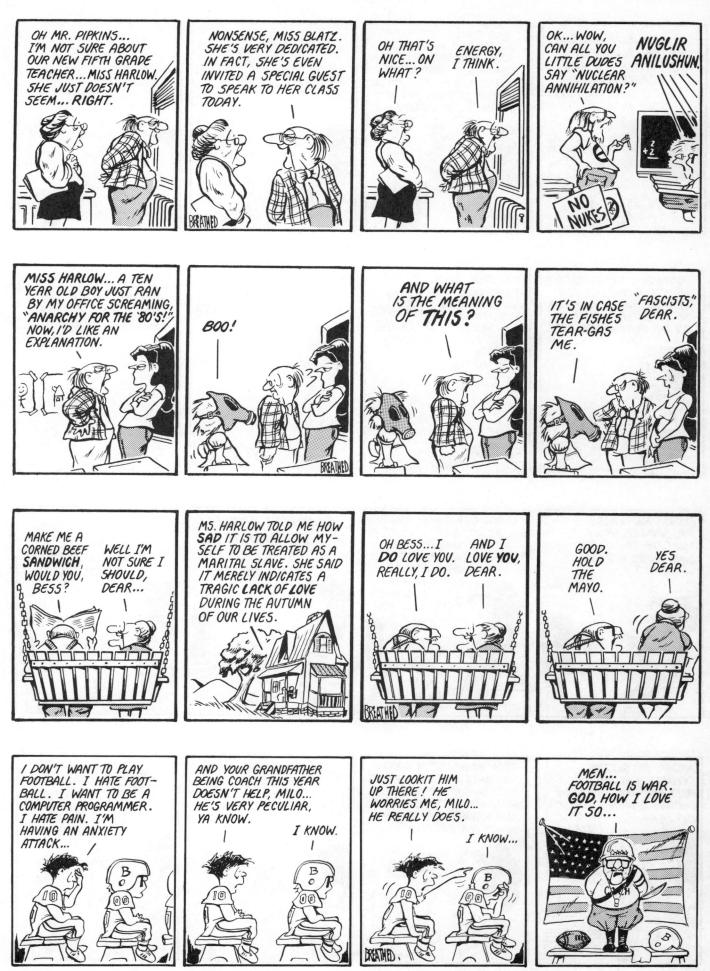

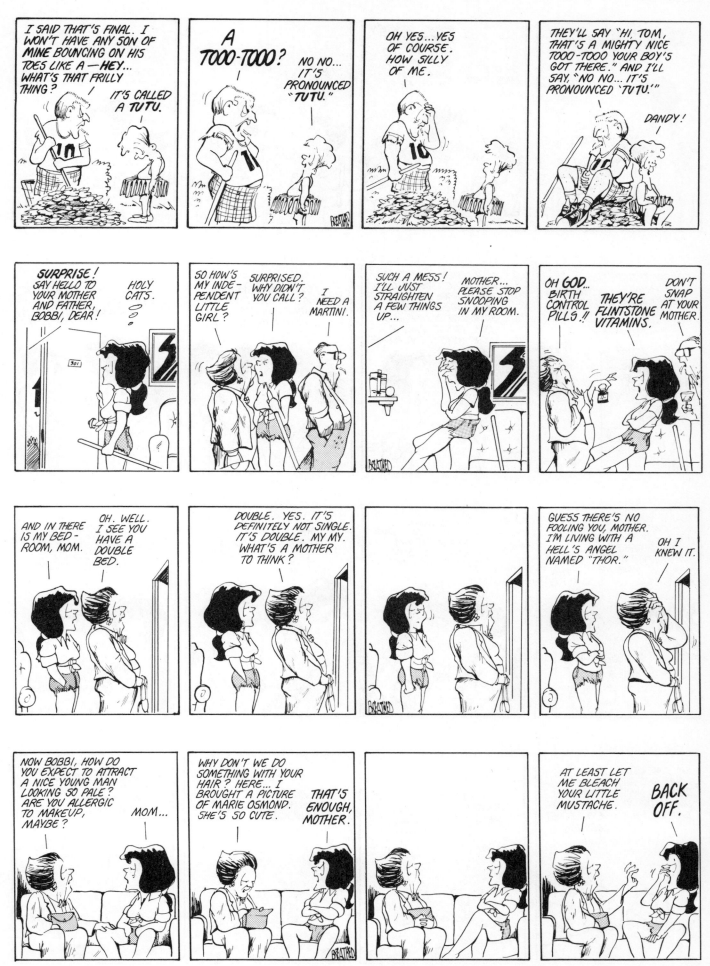

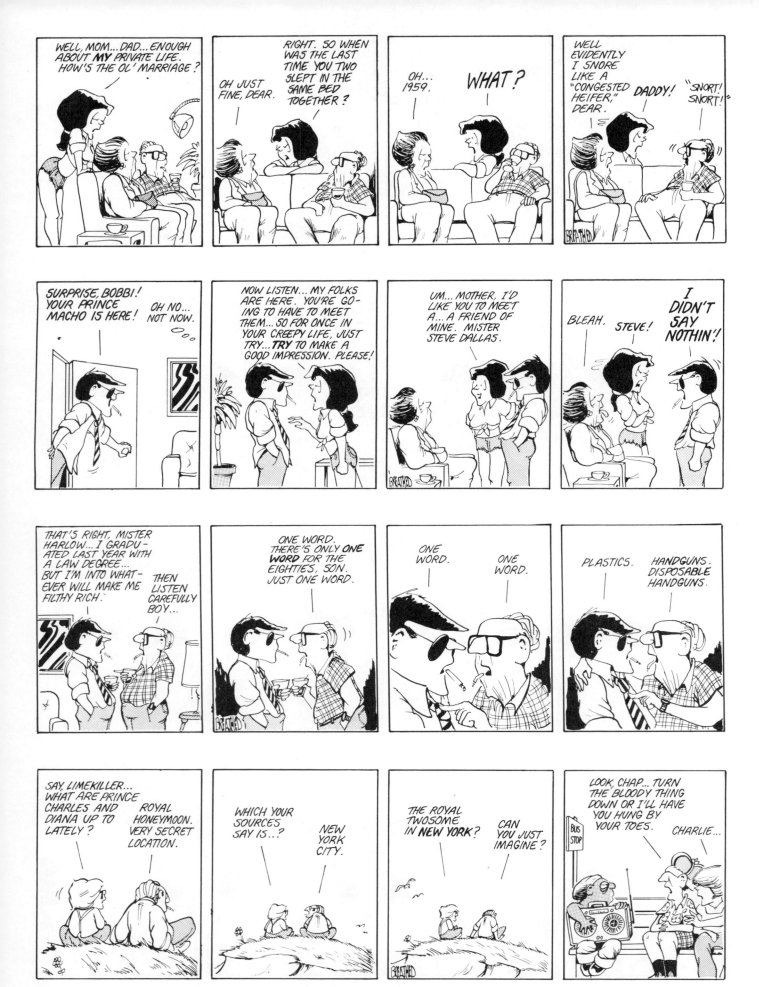

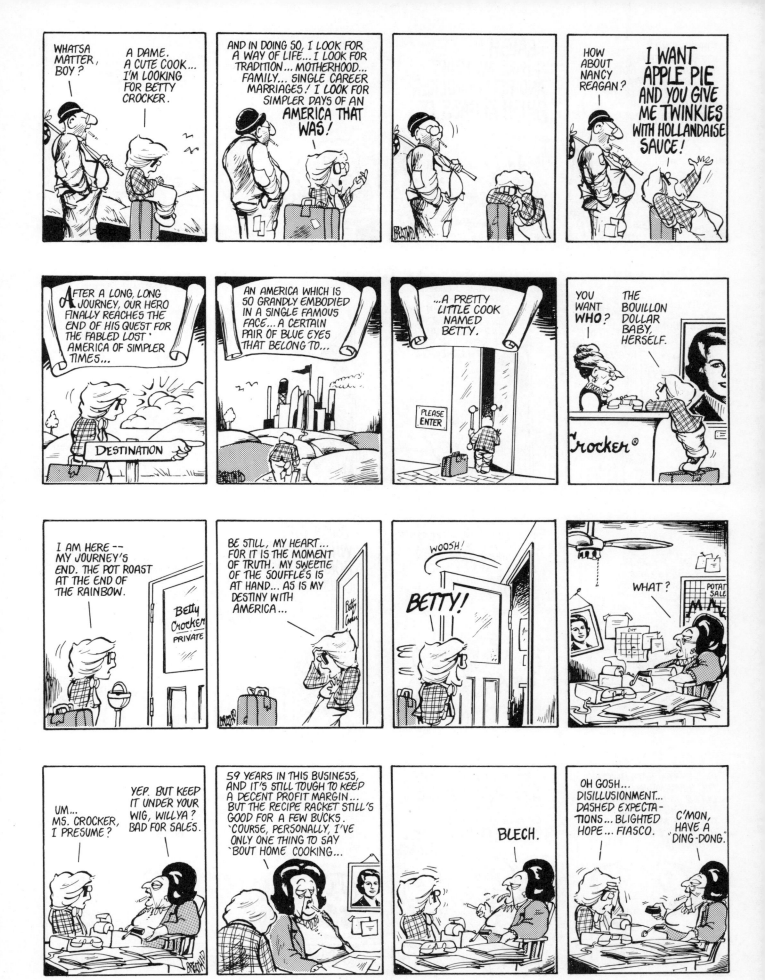

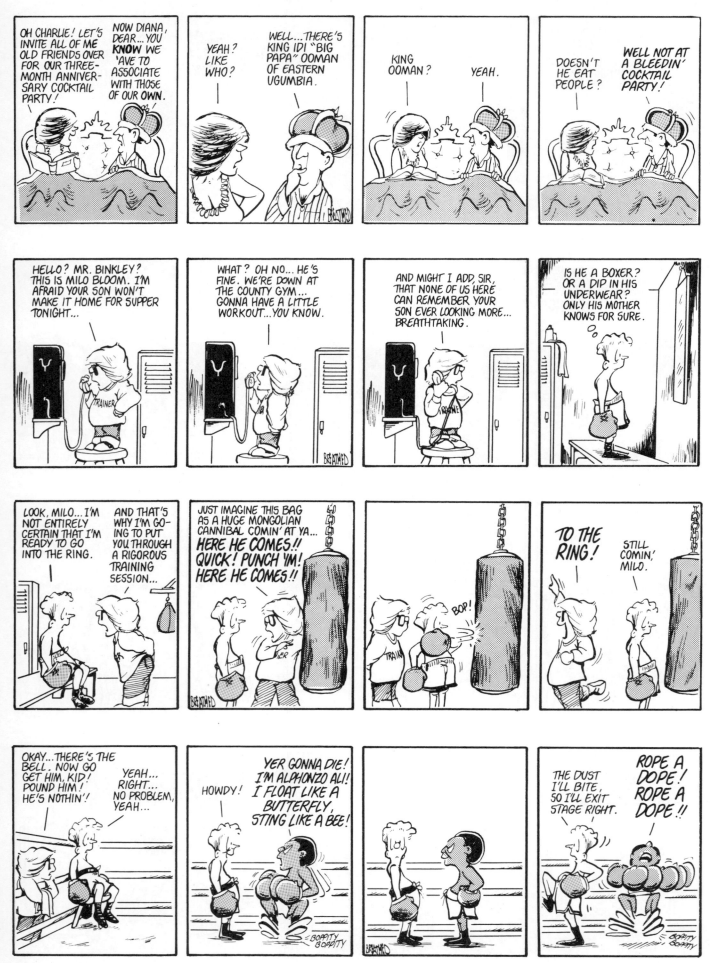

46

54

61

66

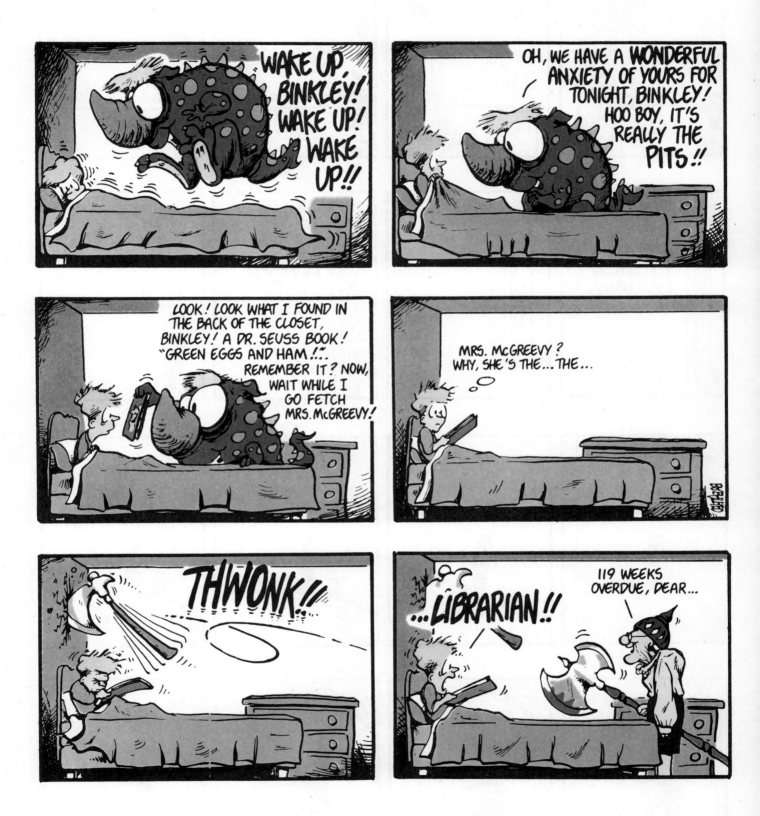

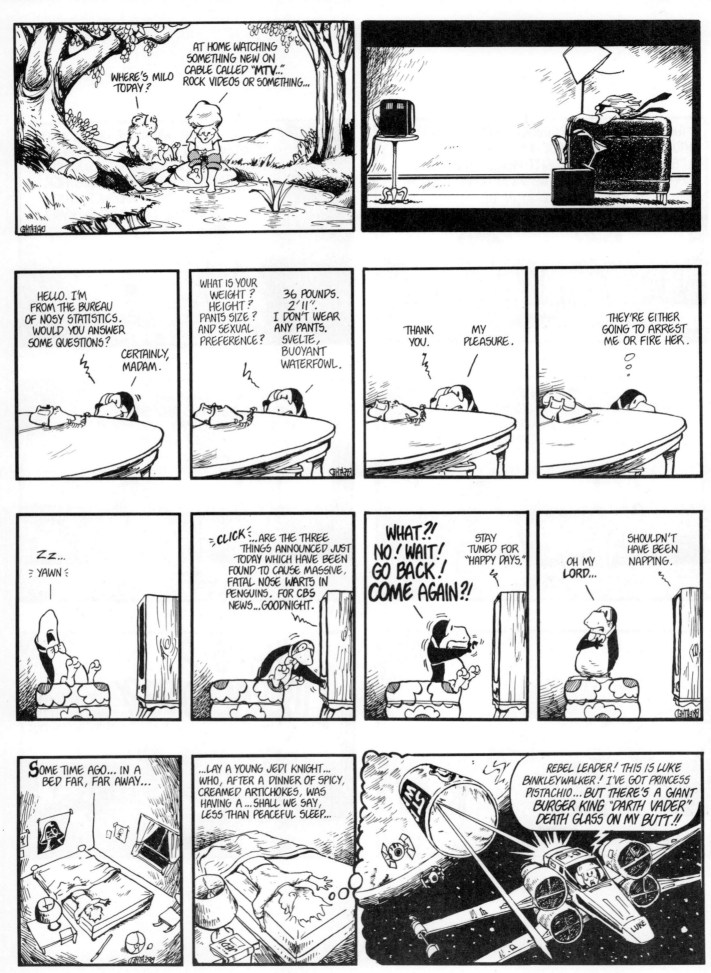

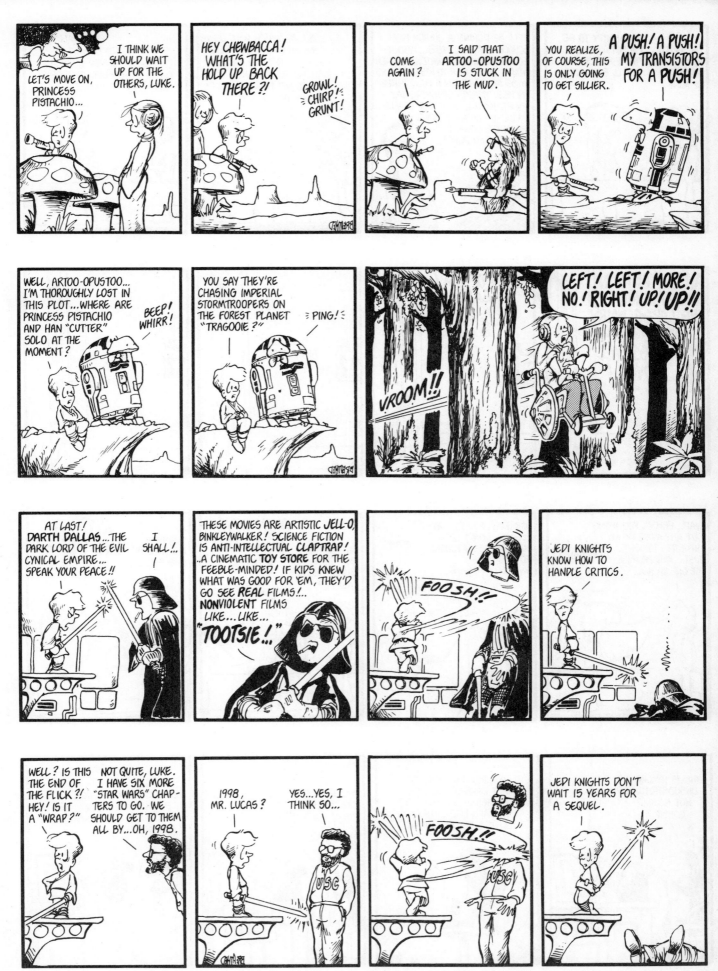

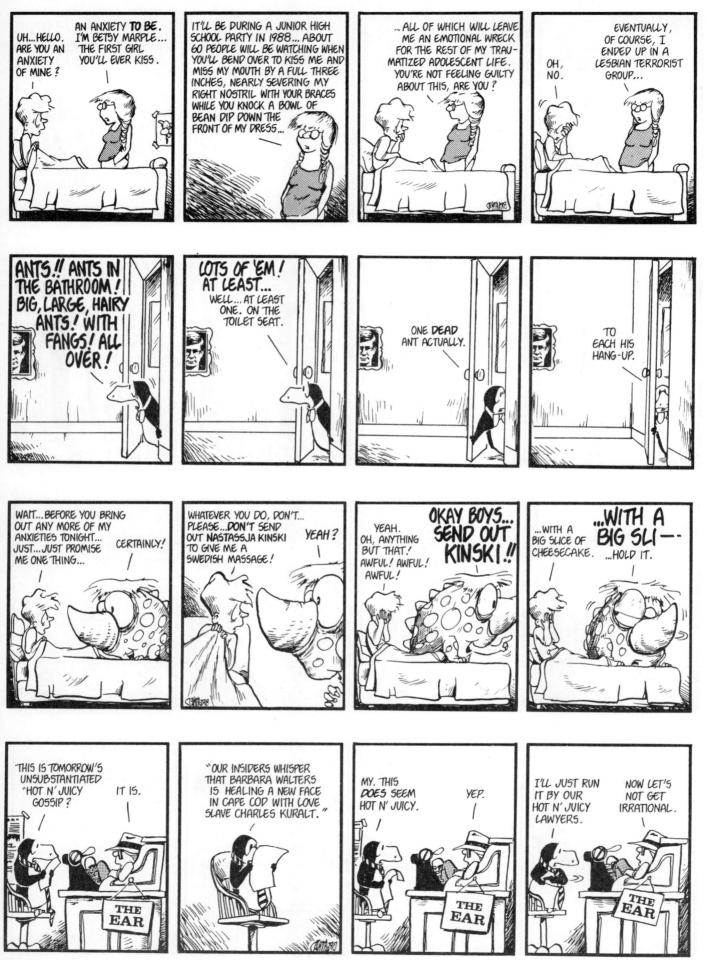

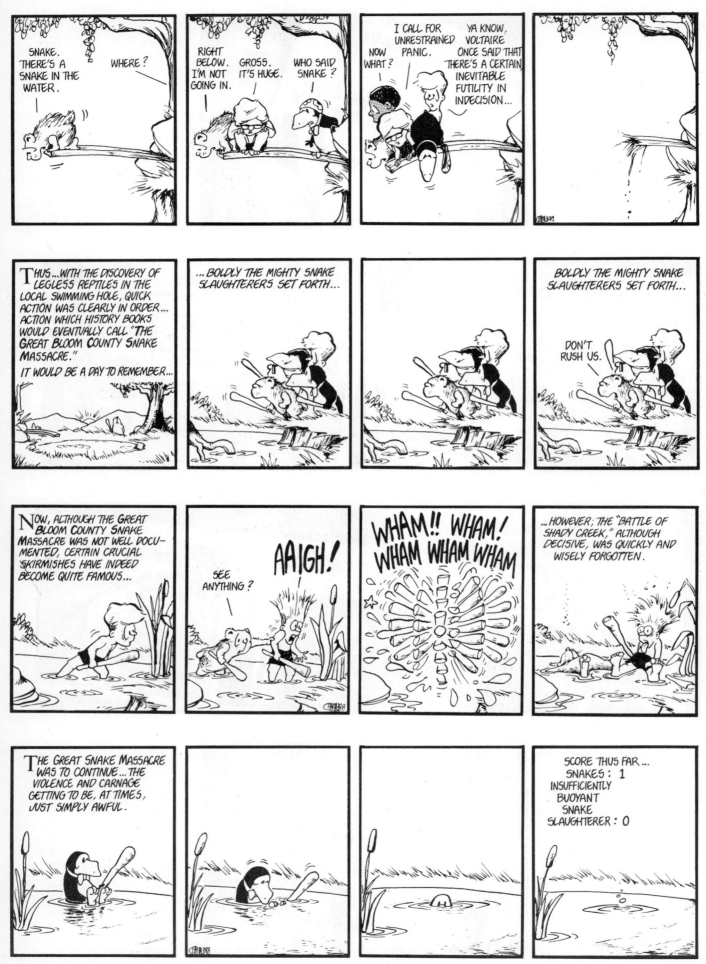

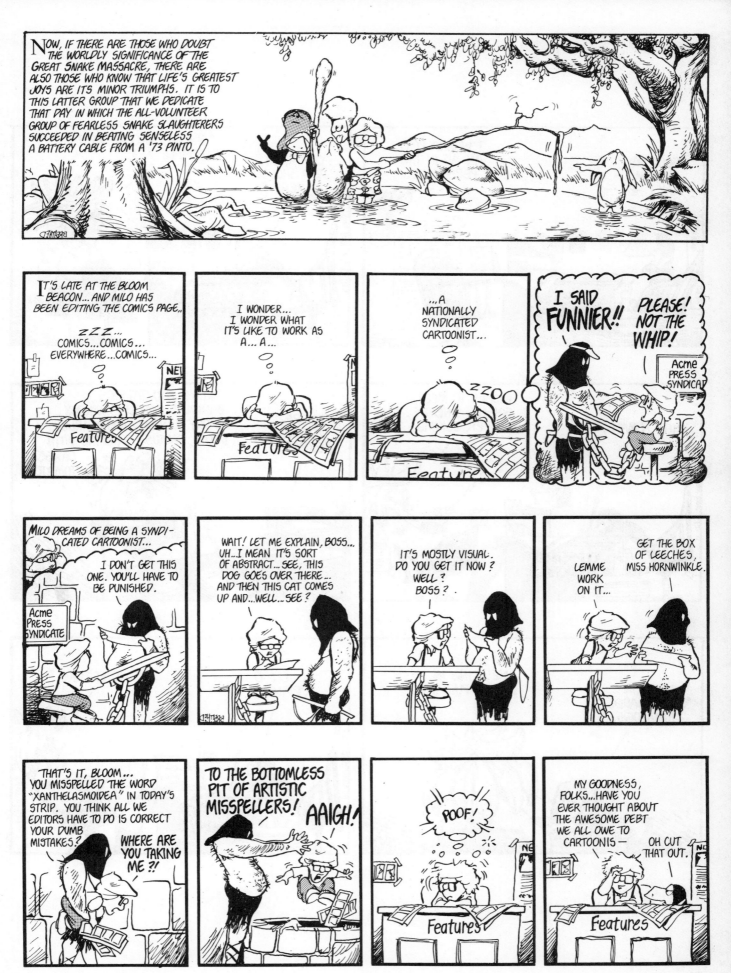

80

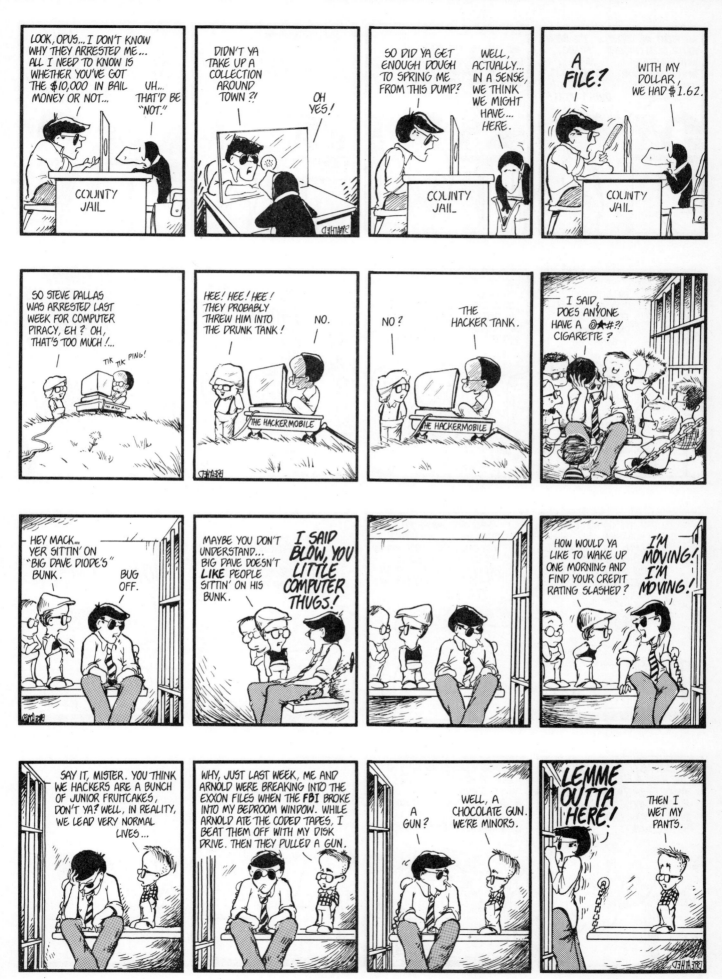

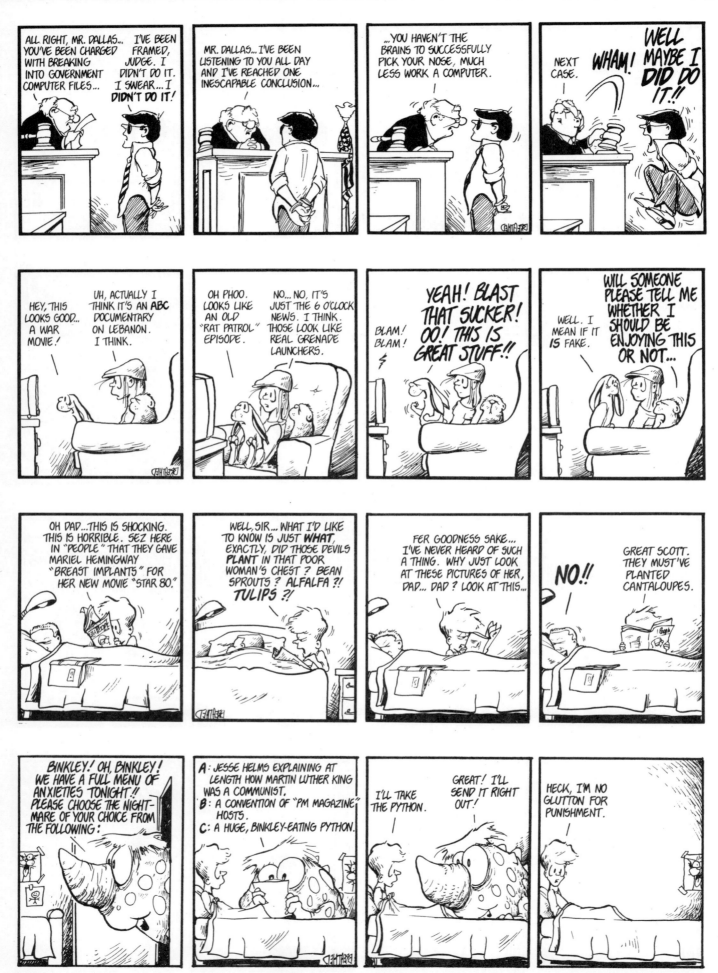

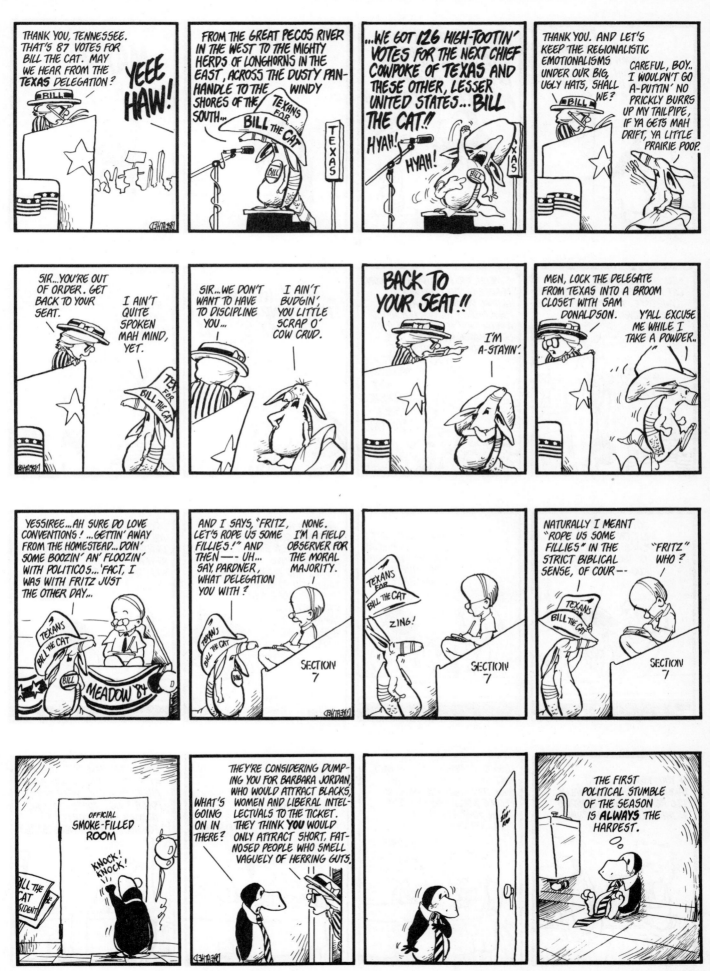

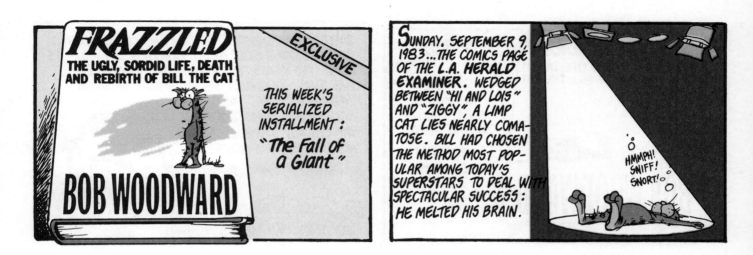

FRAZZLED

THE UGLY, SORDID LIFE, DEATH AND REBIRTH OF BILL THE CAT

BOB WOODWARD

EXCLUSIVE

THIS WEEK'S SERIALIZED INSTALLMENT: "The Fall of a Giant"

SUNDAY, SEPTEMBER 9, 1983...THE COMICS PAGE OF THE L.A. HERALD EXAMINER. WEDGED BETWEEN "HI AND LOIS" AND "ZIGGY", A LIMP CAT LIES NEARLY COMATOSE. BILL HAD CHOSEN THE METHOD MOST POPULAR AMONG TODAY'S SUPERSTARS TO DEAL WITH SPECTACULAR SUCCESS: HE MELTED HIS BRAIN.

HMMPH! SNIFF! SNORT!

THE SAME DAY. WASHINGTON. THE SENATE/COMICS GUILD HEARINGS...

IT'S ALL A MEDIA MYTH, SENATOR. THERE IS NO MORE A DRUG PROBLEM IN THE CARTOON INDUSTRY THAN IN...OH...SAY, THE ENTERTAINMENT INDUSTRY.

WELL! THAT IS A RELIEF!

LATER, SOURCES CLOSE TO BILL WOULD ANONYMOUSLY RECOUNT THE GREAT CAT'S FINAL, SAD DAYS.

ONE DAY HE STARTED CHASING THE GIRLS AROUND THE POOL WITH A PAIR OF ICE TONGS, SCREAMING "PIRANHA!" HE WAS CLEARLY OUT OF CONTROL. THEN HE TOSSED ONE OF THE SWANS INTO THE JACUZZI. HEF NEVER LET BILL INTO THE MANSION AGAIN.

ONE NIGHT BILL SHOWED UP ABOUT 4:00 A.M. AT MY WEST HOLLYWOOD BUNGALOW. HE WAS WHACKED. A MOVIE DEAL JUST FELL THROUGH AND HE WAS UPSET, SO HE THREW A CINDER BLOCK THROUGH THE WINDSHIELD OF MY NEW BMW 533. THEN HE DRANK ALL MY ROOT BEER, STOLE MY MERCEDES AND RAN OVER MY MITT. I NEVER SAW HIM ALIVE AGAIN. I'M VERY DEPRESSED ABOUT THIS.

ALL I KNOW IS THAT RIGHT BEFORE HE WAS KILLED, HE TOLD ME THAT HE BELIEVED HE WOULD COME BACK IN HIS SECOND LIFE AS SHIRLEY MacLAINE. YEP!... THE DRUGS HAD CLEARLY TAKEN THEIR TOLL. AND DON'T USE MY NAME WITH THIS!

NEXT WEEK... "THE FINAL 24 HOURS"

FRAZZLED
THE UGLY, SORDID LIFE, DEATH AND REBIRTH OF BILL THE CAT

EXCLUSIVE

THIS WEEK'S SERIALIZED INSTALLMENT:

"THE LAST 24 HOURS"

BOB WOODWARD

TUESDAY. SEPTEMBER 30TH. 7:16 a.m. A LATE-NIGHT PARTY IN COMIC STAR **MARY WORTH'S** LOS ANGELES HOME. BIG NAMES. BIG MONEY. BIG TEMPTATIONS... **BIG SINS**. IT FINALLY BREAKS UP WITH THE DAWN. "NEED A LIFT HOME?" ASKS SNUFFY SMITH. HE'S NOTICED BILL, WHO LOOKS BAD. "ACK," REPLIES THE CAT AND STUMBLES TOWARD HIS CAR. SMITH SHRUGS.

11:05 a.m. ROUTE 66. EAST TOWARD HOME. BILL'S NERVOUS SYSTEM — RAVAGED BY MONTHS OF CHEMICAL ABUSE — TEETERS PRECARIOUSLY ON THE BRINK OF TOTAL, CATASTROPHIC FAILURE...

SNORT!

HIGH NOON. THE OUTSKIRTS OF BLOOM COUNTY. 143 M.P.H. OBLIVION...DEAD AHEAD...THE PIPER IS ABOUT TO BE PAID...

VROOOM!! VROOOM!!

CACTUS AHEAD

SCREEEEECH!! OOOOO

BILL

7:43 p.m. A SCENE OF TOTAL AUTOMOTIVE DEVASTATION. A LONE AND SORROWFUL FIGURE DISCOVERS THAT OF THE ONCE GLORIOUS BILL THE CAT...NOT ONE SCRAP REMAINS. NOT ONE SINGLE, SOLITARY PIECE... EXCEPT...

GREAT SCOTT! IT'S HIS...HIS...

NEXT WEEK: THE SHOCKING SECRET

DIFF'RENT STROKES

WILL RETURN IN A MINUTE!

OH. YES...HELLO! WELCOME TO THE AMERICAN MEADOW PARTY'S FIRST AND ONLY POLITICAL COMMERCIAL... ON WHICH, I'M TOLD, WE'VE BLOWN ALL OF OUR REMAINING DOUGH.

AHEM. WE OFFER NO WILD PROMISES. WE ONLY OFFER OURSELVES. BILL, HERE, IS A FORMER MISSIONARY. I AM STUDYING TO BE THE POPE. OUR VALUES ARE SUPERB. WE WANT YOUR VOTE.

SOME SAY WE'RE DESPERATE. NOT TRUE! WE PLEDGE NEVER TO STOOP TO UNSAVORY PETTY POLITICKING WITH THE TWO FRONTRUNNERS...

NAMELY, THE DEMOCRATIC CANDIDATE, SEEN HERE IN A 1972 PHOTO WITH MADALYN MURRAY O'HAIR AT AN "UP WITH ATHEISTS" BANQUET...

...AND THE REPUBLICAN CANDIDATE, SEEN HERE IN A 1959 PHOTO SHARING A SMOKE AND REMINISCING WITH ROOMMATE AND FORMER FRAT BROTHER FIDEL "STOGIE" CASTRO.

AND SO NEXT TUESDAY, THINK OF US...AND THINK OF THEM. THE "BEAK AND SALIVA TICKET"... GO FOR IT! THANK YOU.

BiLL + OPUS FOR 1984 This time, Why not the Worst?

AND NOW, MORE DIFF'RENT STROKES

PHZZZZ...
=CRACKLE=

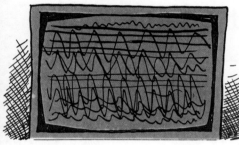

WE INTERRUPT THIS PROGRAM FOR A SPECIAL MESSAGE FROM THE UNITED STATES FEDERAL ELECTION COMMISSION...

ON OCTOBER 28TH, THE AMERICAN MEADOW PARTY BROADCAST A PAID POLITICAL COMMERCIAL NARRATED BY THEIR V.P. CANDIDATE SHOWN HERE.

GULP!

POLITICAL DISTORTIONIST

THE COMMERCIAL INCLUDED TWO PHOTO-GRAPHS APPARENTLY SHOWING RONALD REAGAN AND WALTER MONDALE IN CLOSE ASSOCIATION WITH FIDEL CASTRO AND MADALYN MURRAY O'HAIR, RESPECTIVELY.

I'M NOT RESPONSIBLE! REALLY!

THE COMMISSION HAS LEARNED THAT THE PHOTOS HAD BEEN TAMPERED WITH.

THEM! THEY MADE ME DO IT! MY ADVISORS! THEM! THEM! THEM!

POLITICAL DISTORTIONIST

THE FOLLOWING ARE THE GENUINE, UN-DOCTORED PHOTOS WHICH CLEARLY SHOW WHO THE CANDIDATES WERE ACTUALLY APPEARING WITH...

POLITICAL DISTORTIONIST

"BULLWINKLE..."

AND "PUGSLEY" FROM "THE ADDAMS FAMILY".

WE HOPE THOSE RESPONSIBLE FULLY REALIZE JUST EXACTLY HOW MUCH TROUBLE THEY'RE IN.

OH, THEY DO, MAN, THEY DO!

POLITICAL

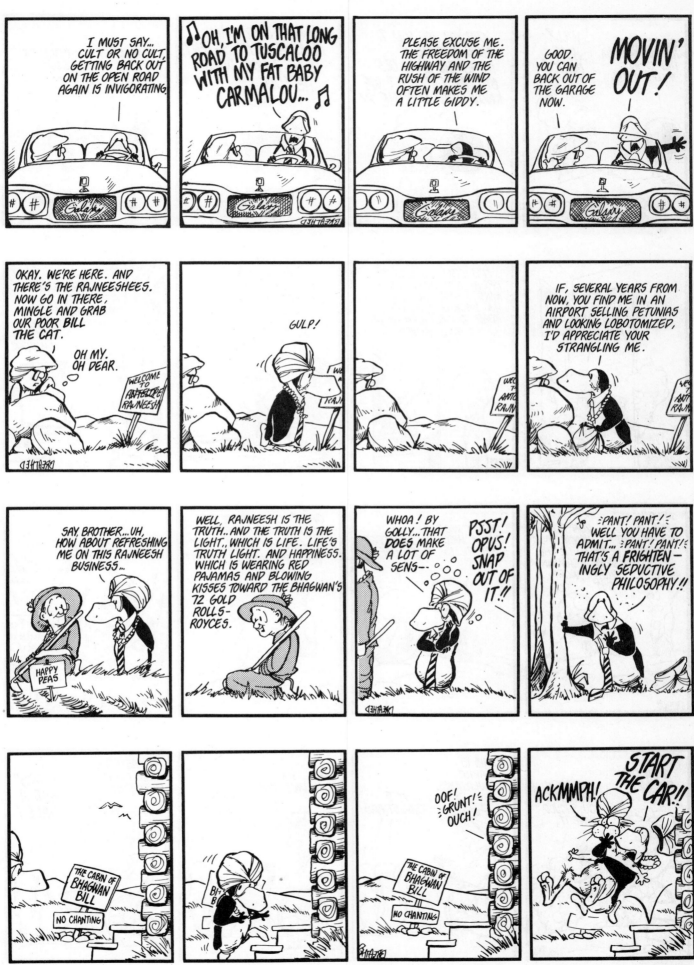

~11:09 p.m. Cygnus 17 appears normal.
—11:23 p.m. No activity on Jupiter's 3rd moon.
—11:40 p.m. The western sky is looking particularly ...empty.
...in fact, the entire universe is appearing every bit the meaningless and cold vacuum that it is... Where Truth is relative, God elusive, and Man just an insignificant blob of cosmic spittle.
SIGH
—11:51 P.M. Retreats to go listen to a few old Reagan speeches for dramatic renewal of purpose.

114

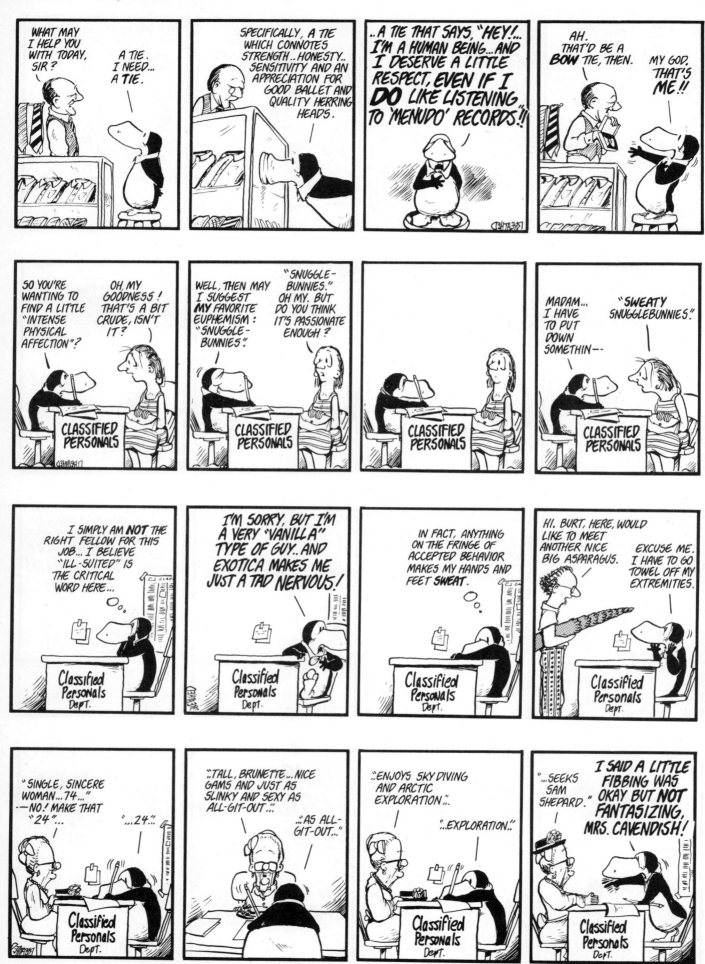

118

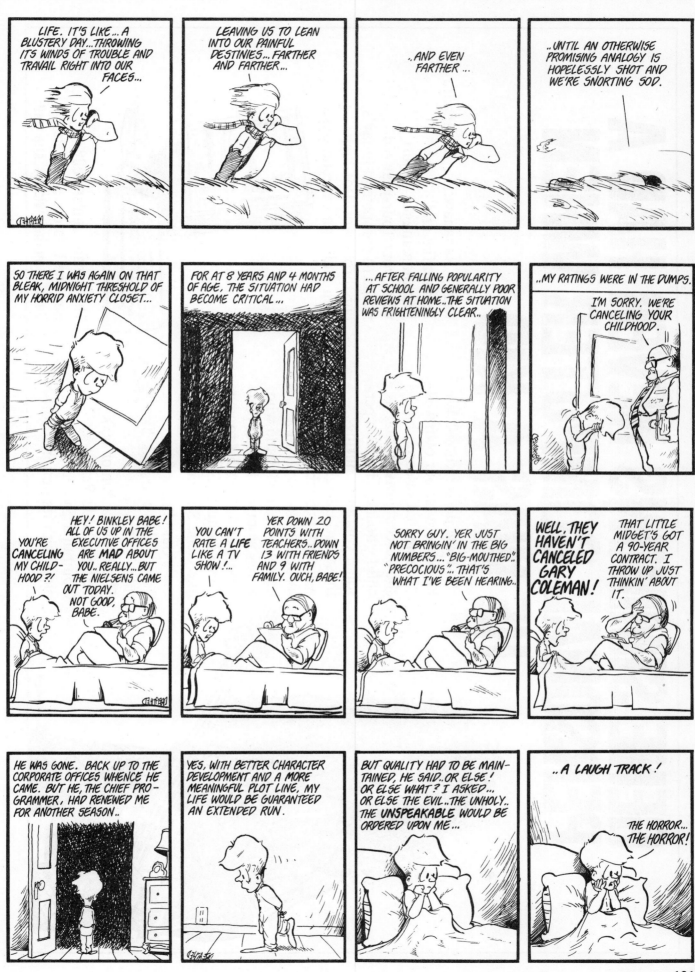

GENE SIMMONS NEVER HAD A PERSONAL COMPUTER WHEN HE WAS A KID

How do we know? We know because our own well-documented research has shown conclusively that a child who lacks his own personal computer during those earliest school years will very probably grow up to be a bass player in a heavy-metal rock band who wears women's fishnet pantyhose and sticks his tongue down to his kneecaps. Just like Gene Simmons.

Your child's future doesn't have to look like this.

The Banana Junior 6000 Self-portable Personal Computer System, complete with its optional software— Bananawrite, Bananadraw, Bananafile and Bananamanager—is just what your four-year-old needs to compete in today's cut-throat world of high tech and high expectations.

**The Banana Junior 6000...
Buy one before it's too late.
Gene's mother wishes she had.**

123

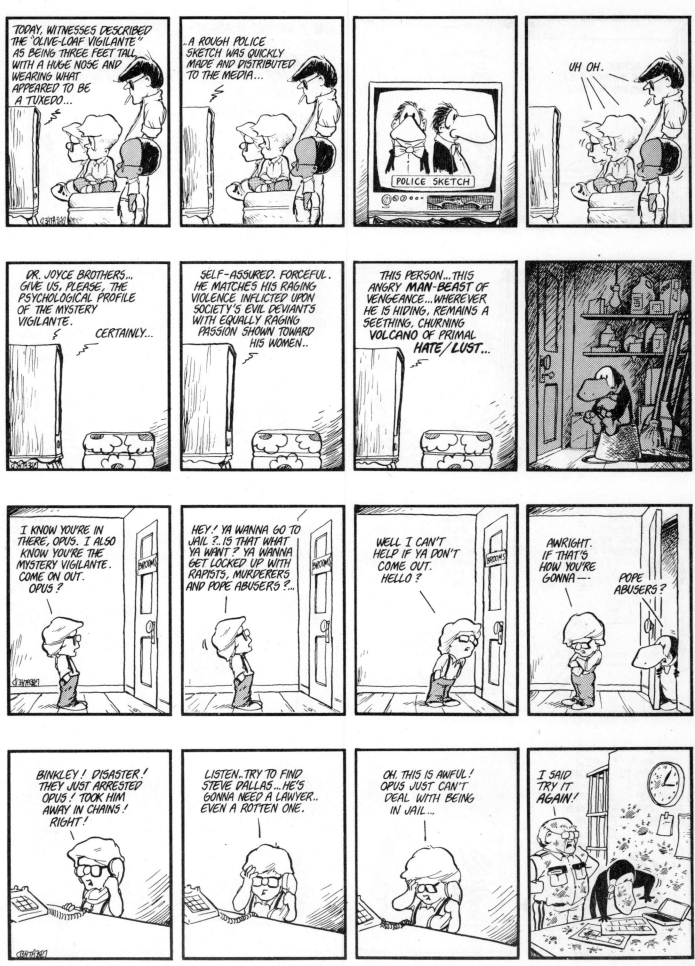

126

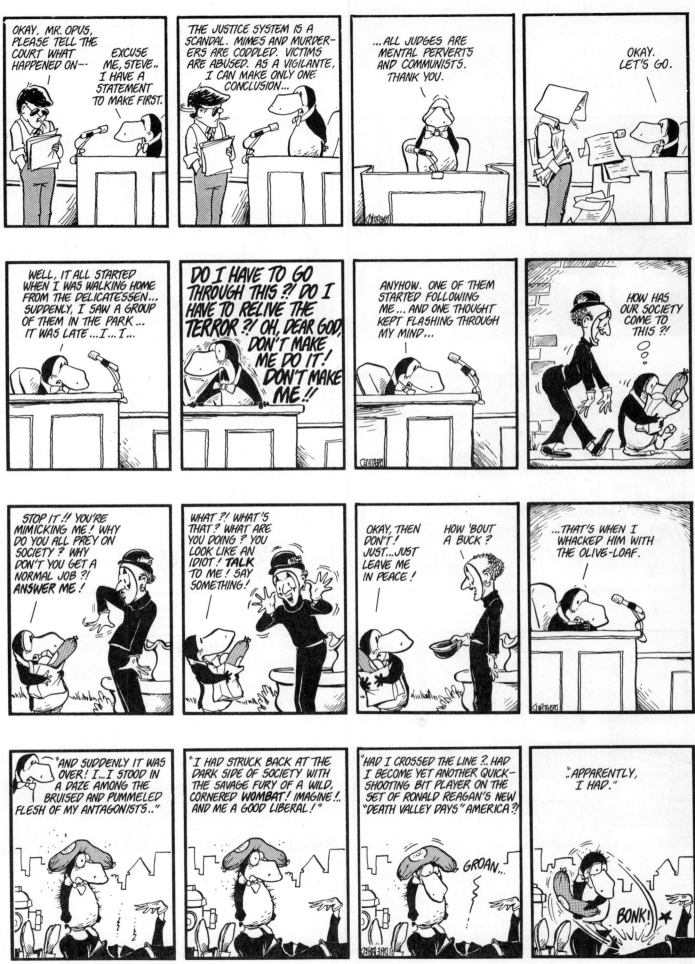

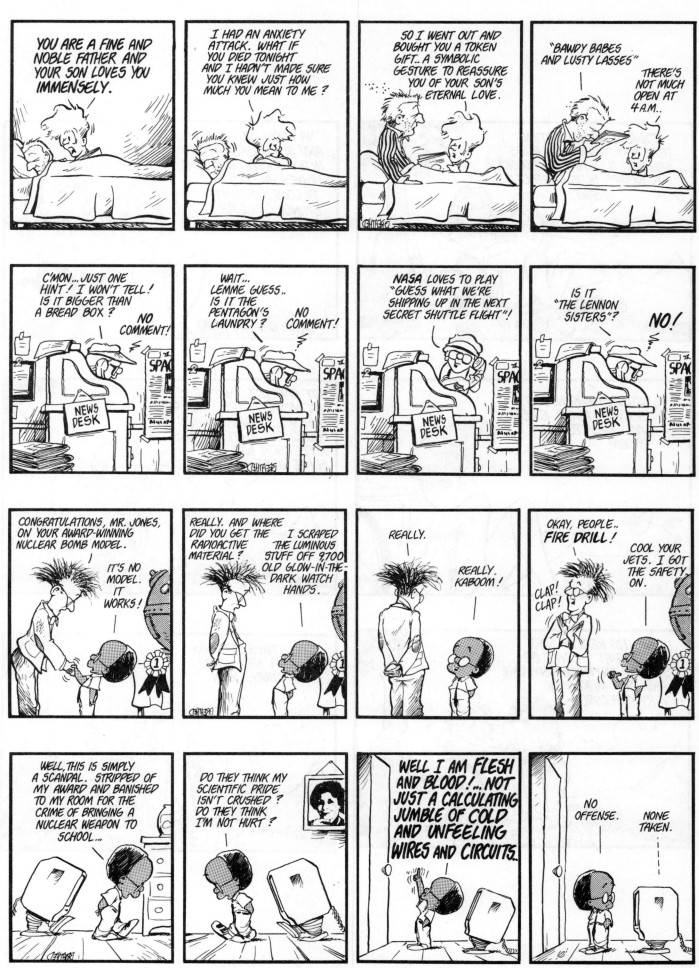

133

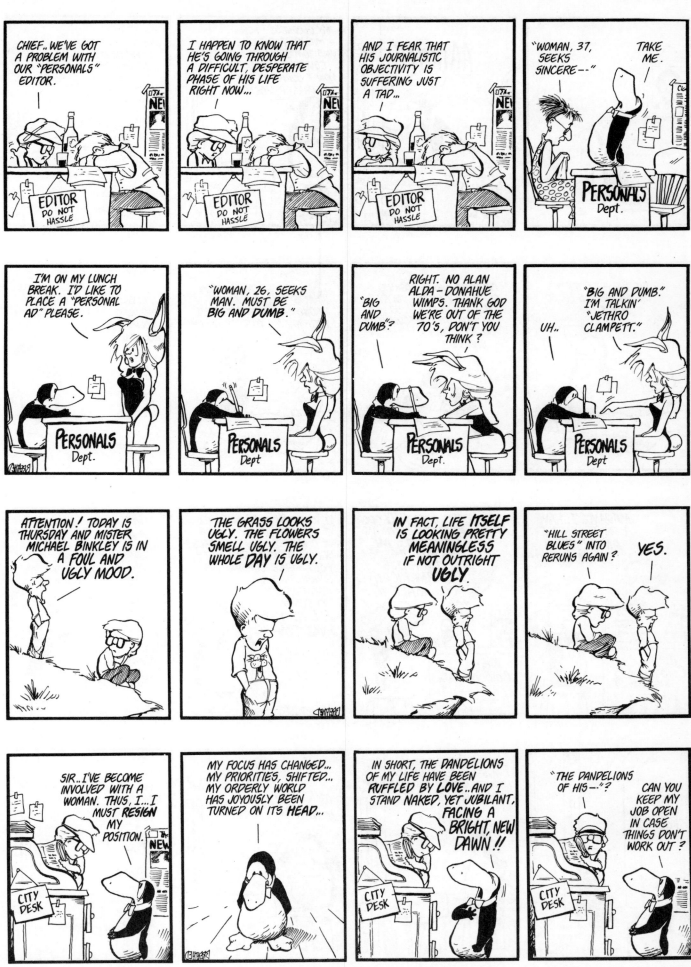

137

138

140

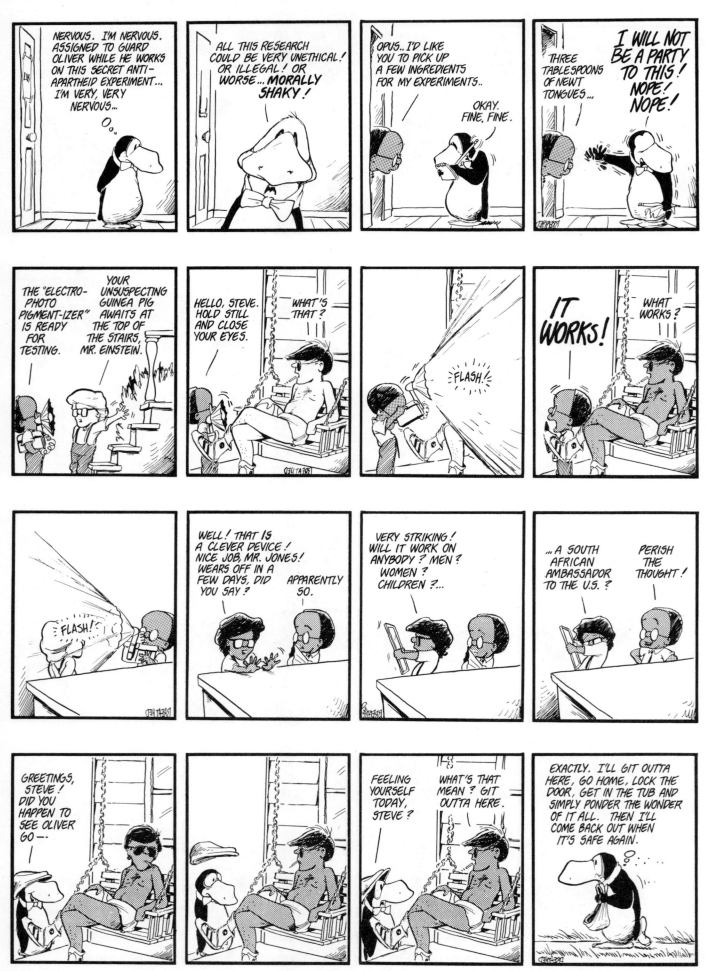

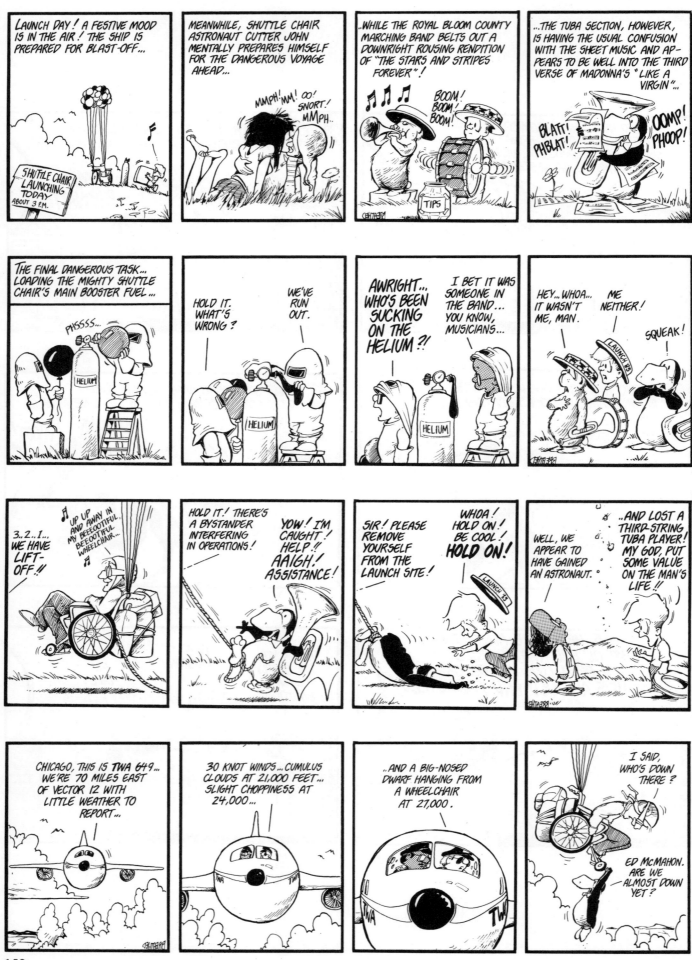

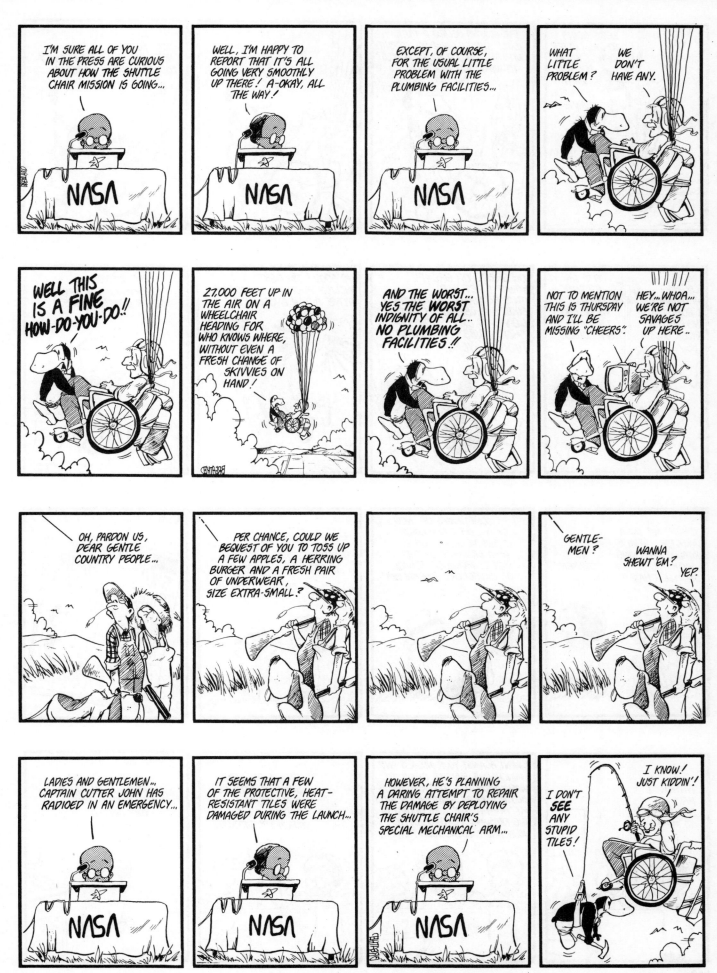

151

154

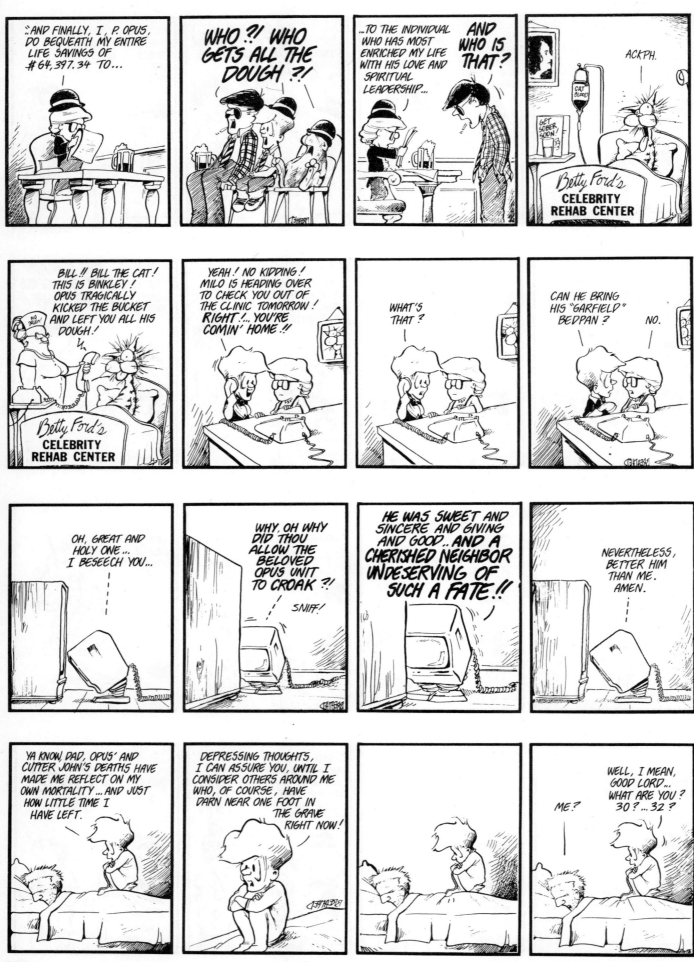

156

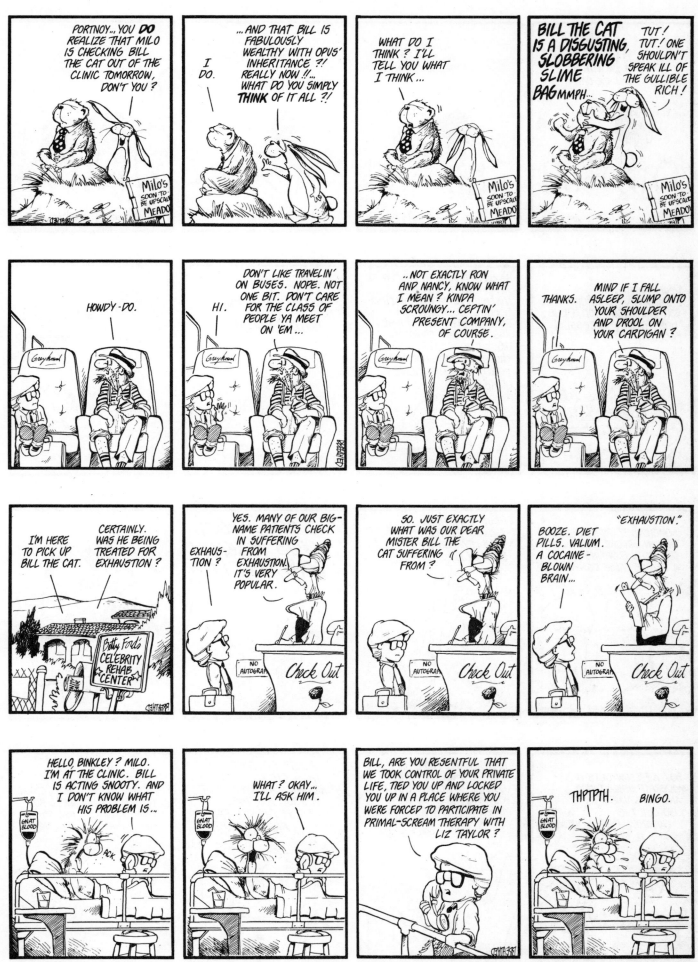

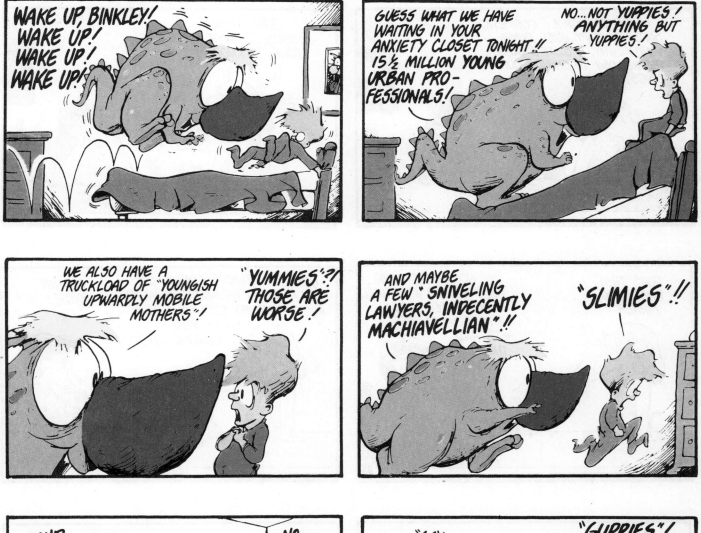

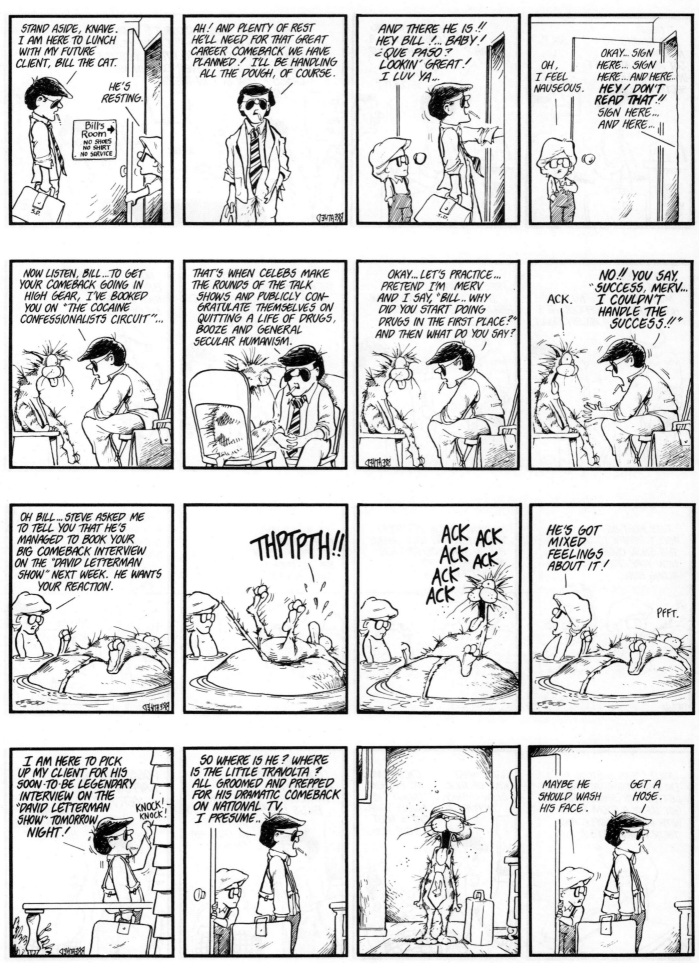

164

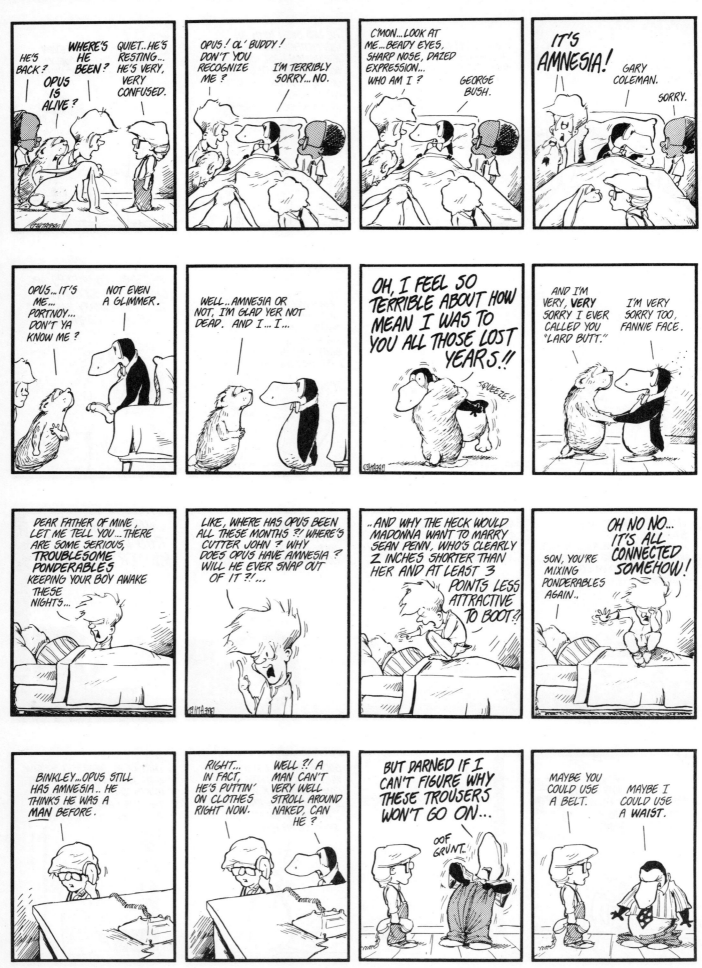

168

172

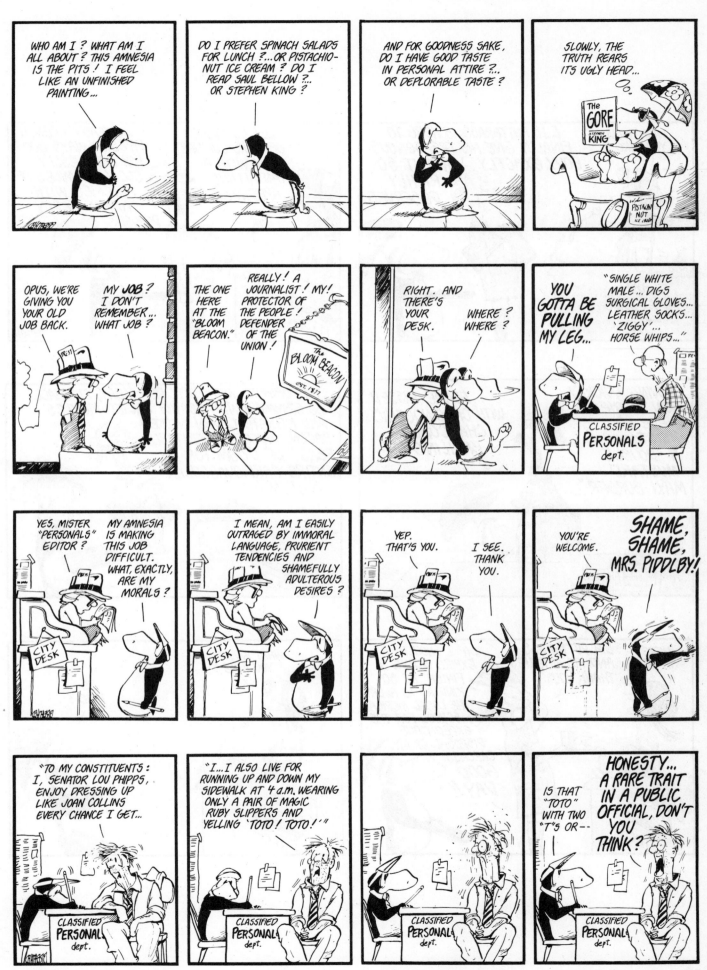

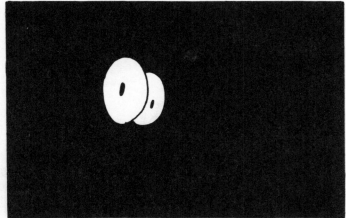

178

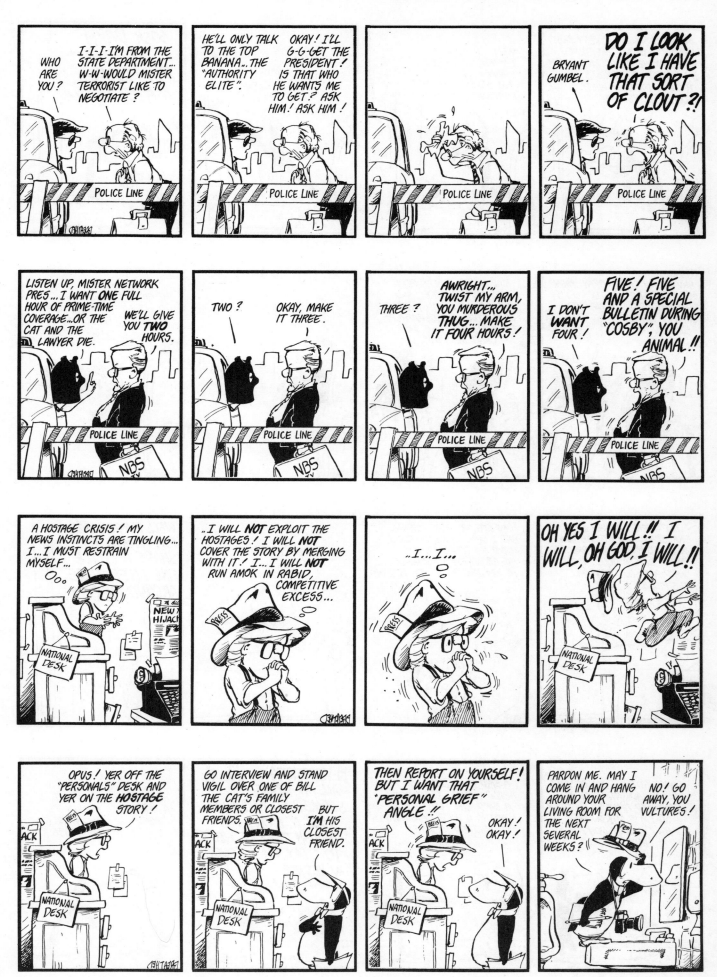

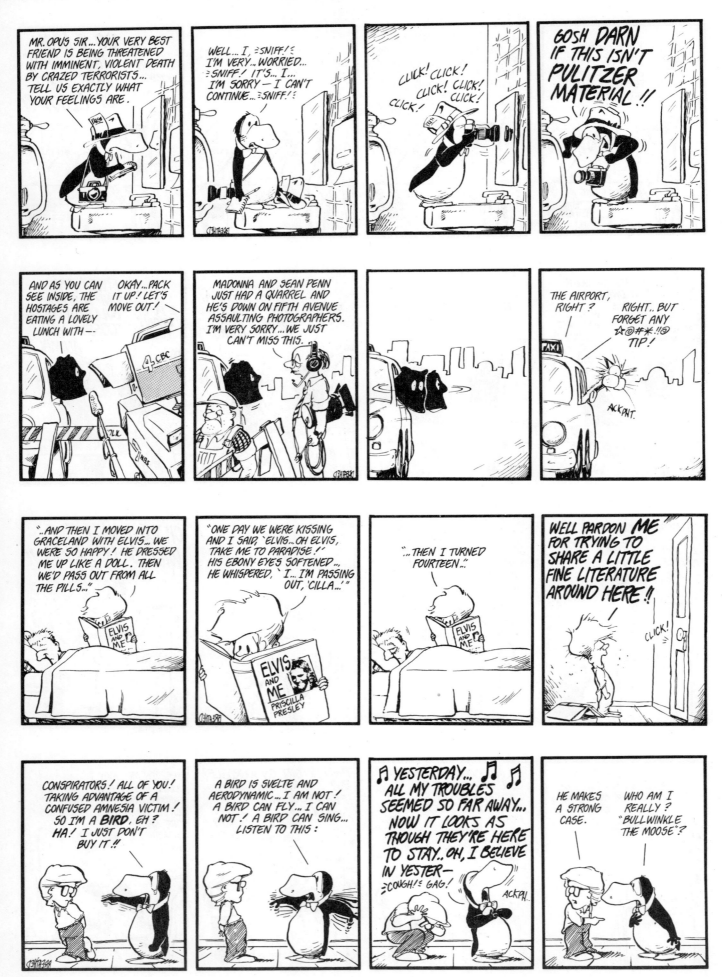

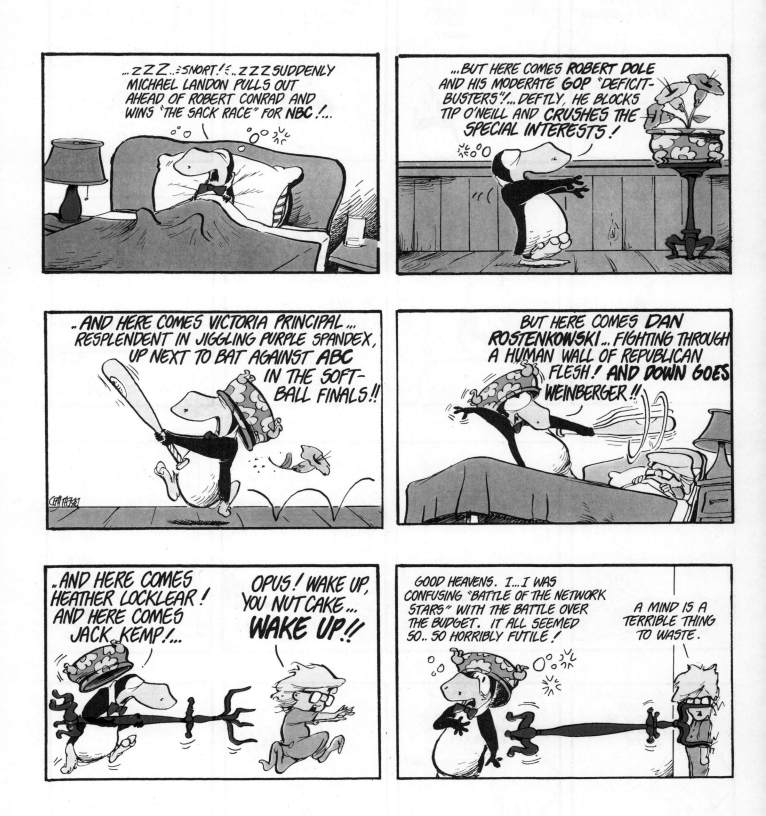

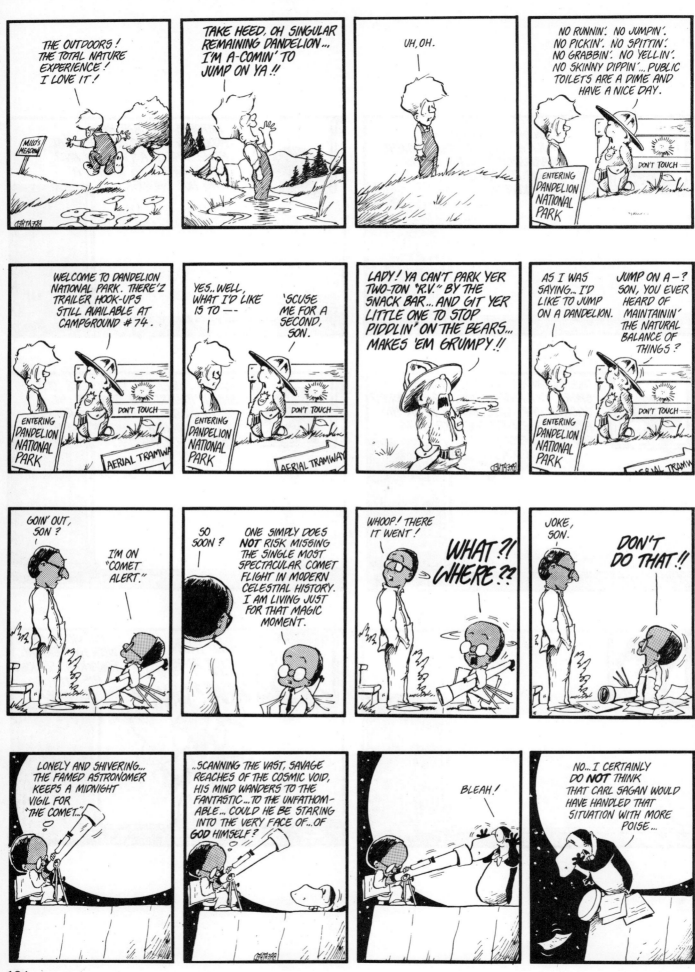

184

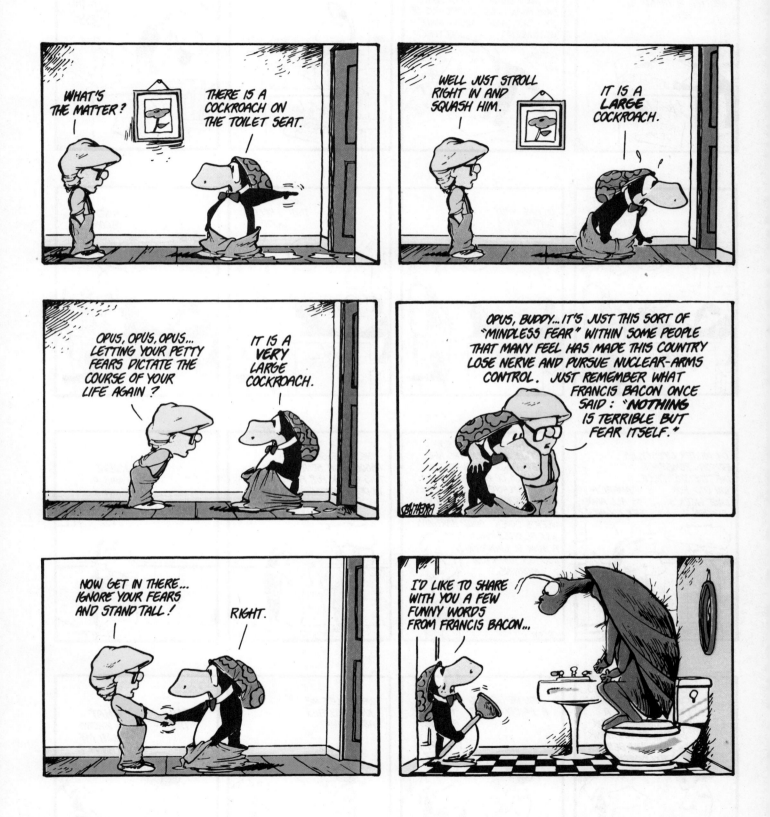

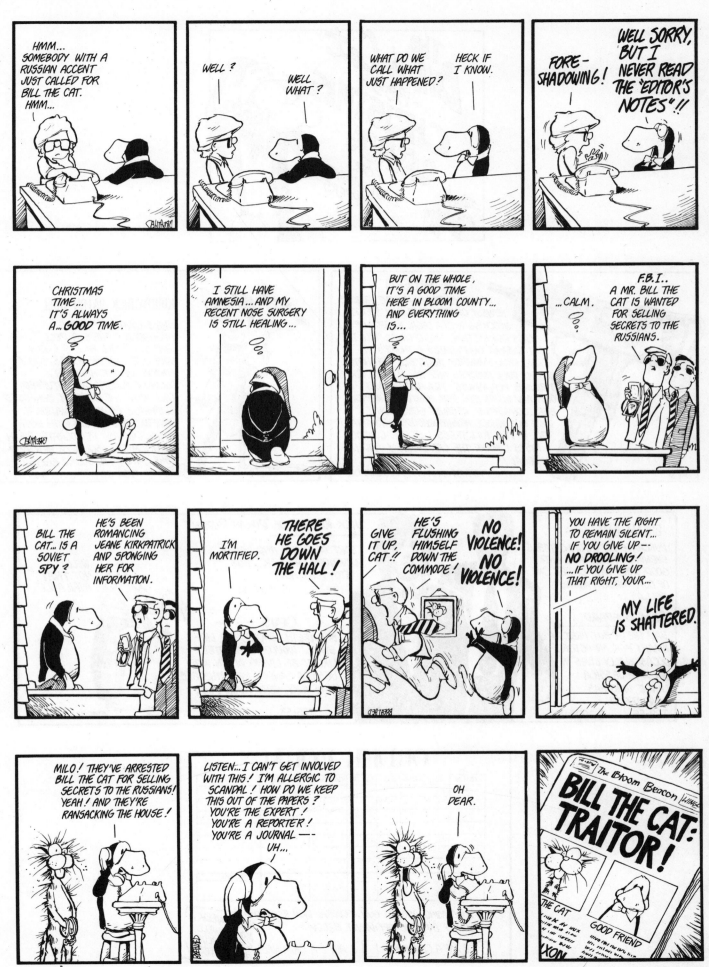

The Bill the Cat
—1985—
CHRISTMAS CATALOG
FOR LAST-MINUTE SHOPPERS

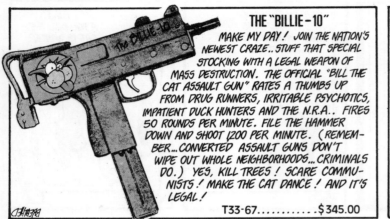

THE "BILLIE-10"

MAKE MY DAY! JOIN THE NATION'S NEWEST CRAZE.. STUFF THAT SPECIAL STOCKING WITH A LEGAL WEAPON OF MASS DESTRUCTION. THE OFFICIAL "BILL THE CAT ASSAULT GUN" RATES A THUMBS UP FROM DRUG RUNNERS, IRRITABLE PSYCHOTICS, IMPATIENT DUCK HUNTERS AND THE N.R.A.. FIRES 50 ROUNDS PER MINUTE. FILE THE HAMMER DOWN AND SHOOT 1200 PER MINUTE. (REMEMBER...CONVERTED ASSAULT GUNS DON'T WIPE OUT WHOLE NEIGHBORHOODS...CRIMINALS DO.) YES, KILL TREES! SCARE COMMUNISTS! MAKE THE CAT DANCE! AND IT'S LEGAL!

T33-67...........$345.00

KIRKPATRICK PATCH DOLL

SHE'S LOVABLE! SHE'S HUGGABLE! SHE'S A DOLL!... AND SHE'S ALL BILL'S! BUT NOW SHE CAN BE YOURS, TOO! FORMED OF THE HARDEST, COLDEST PLASTIC AND STUFFED FULL WITH THE SOFTEST SHREDDED CLIPPINGS FROM THE "NATIONAL REVIEW", SHE COMES WITH BOTH REPUBLICAN AND DEMOCRATIC BIRTH CERTIFICATES. SQUEEZE HER AND SHE SAYS "U.N. SUCKS EGGS!"

T34-78...........$49.95

DREAM DATE

PURCHASE AN UNFORGETTABLE EVENING OF ROMANCE AND GOOD WINE WITH EITHER ONE OF OUR THREE FANTASY FELLAS...

SAM SHEPARD →

BAD TEETH BUT PRETTY SMART FOR AN ACTOR. OCCASIONALLY LIVES IN SIN WITH JESSICA LANGE, WHO HAS FINE TEETH.
T89-66......$2000.00

← NICK RHODES OF "DURAN DURAN"

SORT OF SHORT AND WEARS LAVENDER LIPSTICK...BUT VERY, VERY HOT.
T78-45.... $2500.00

OPUS →

BAD TEETH. SHORT. NO LIPSTICK. WOULD DESPERATELY LIKE TO BE LIVING IN SIN WITH JESSICA LANGE. NEVERTHELESS, HE IS VERY, VERY AVAILABLE.
T65-53......$9.95

WELL, NOT *THAT* AVAILABLE.

FOR RENT

ORDER FORM

ITEM #	ITEM NAME	SIZE	COLOR	CALIBER	ITEM PRICE	TOTAL PRICE
						TOTAL

IF PURCHASING ASSAULT GUN, FEDERAL LAW REQUIRES FILLING OUT THE AFFIDAVIT BELOW:

☐ I AM A CRIMINAL.   ☐ I AIN'T A CRIMINAL.

NEXT WEEK.. MORE SWELL GIFTS! PLUS— BIG CONTEST!

209

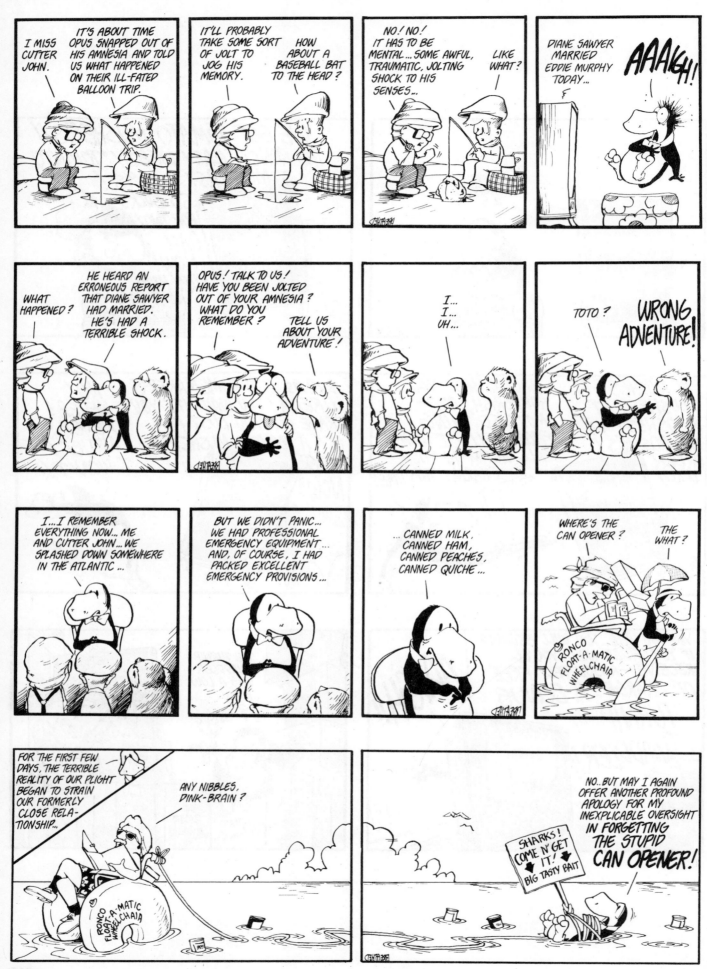

216

218

219

The Official Results of BILL'S BIG ART CONTEST

GRAND PRIZES: BILL DOLLS

-NO- GOOD HOUSEKEEPING SEAL OF APPROVAL

THE 27,366 DRAWINGS WE RECEIVED WERE BROKEN DOWN INTO THE FOLLOWING THEMES...

JUDGE

ENTRIES

Theme	%
BILL DRUNK	6%
BILL ELECTROCUTED	3%
BILL WITH FIREARMS	4%
BILL EXPOSING HIMSELF	2%
BILL IMPALED ON XMAS TREE	9%
BILL EATING GARFIELD	1%
GARFIELD EATING BILL	1%
SCATOLOGICAL THEMES	5%
SEXUAL THEMES	4%
BILL SPITTING HAIRBALLS AT BROOKE SHIELDS	11%
— AT GEORGE MICHAEL OF "WHAM!"	15%
— AT DON JOHNSON'S CHEST	12%
— AT ANY PART OF GEORGE BUSH	23%
OTHER	4%

HONORABLE MENTION "BEST"

"BILL STUFFS A CHRISTMAS TURKEY" BY SUSANNA CROSBY OF LA JOLLA, CALIFORNIA.

JUDGES: "WELL DONE. SENSITIVE...BUT NOT OVERBEARING. WE WERE DEEPLY MOVED."

HONORABLE MENTION "WORST"

"BILL - A TREE STAND" BY RICHARD LANDESMAN OF COLCHESTER, VT.

JUDGES: "SICKENING. WARPED. MR. LANDESMAN HAS OBVIOUSLY BEEN LISTENING TO HEAVY METAL ROCK MUSIC."

GRAND PRIZE WINNERS

THWAP! HIC! HIC!

← WORST

"BILL AT THE WHITE HOUSE CHRISTMAS PARTY" BY ROBERT HOCH OF WHITE PLAINS, N.Y.

JUDGES: "BREATHTAKING IN ITS TASTELESSNESS. THE PRESIDENT OF THE WORLD'S MOST POWERFUL AND MORAL NATION DESERVES MORE RESPECT THAN THIS. MONUMENTALLY INEXCUSABLE. THE ARTIST WINS A BILL DOLL."

BEST →

"UNTITLED" BY MISS NICOLE TOWNLEY OF PUEBLO, CO.

JUDGES: "SUPERBLY MINIMALIST! SPARSE IN HER USE OF LINE AND FORM, MS. TOWNLEY — ALREADY A MATURE ABSTRACT EXPRESSIONIST AT AGE FIVE, HAS BRILLIANTLY CAPTURED THE MAGIC...THE GLORY...THE WONDER OF A CAT NAMED BILL."

BILL

POSSIBLY AN ELF. OR A BUG. OR "PRINCE"